TWENTIETH-CENTURY

MONTANA:

A STATE OF EXTREMES

TWENTIETH-CENTURY MONTANA

A STATE OF EXTREMES

By K. ROSS TOOLE

UNIVERSITY OF OKLAHOMA PRESS

NORMAN

By K. Ross Toole

A History of Montana. 2 vols. New York, 1957
Historical Essays on Montana and the Northwest. (Ed., with
    J. W. Smurr). Helena, Montana, 1957
Montana: An Uncommon Land. Norman, 1959.
Probing the American West. (Ed.). Santa Fe, 1960.
An Angry Man Talks Up to Youth. New York, 1970.
The Time Has Come. New York, 1971.
Twentieth-Century Montana: A State of Extremes. Norman,
    1972.

International Standard Book Number: 0–8061–0992–0

Library of Congress Catalog Card Number: 75–177348

This Book Is Dedicated to the
Members Past and Present of my Seminar
History 598: Montana and the West

INTRODUCTION

THIS book is not a history of twentieth-century Montana. Such a book would be valuable, indeed, but this is not it. I doubt that such a history, balanced and "definitive," will be written for a long time. The sources are simply not yet available.

This book is a kind of "portrait" of cyclical twentieth-century patterns in Montana. Even as a "portrait," it is partial because, presumably, a portrait painter (at least a good one) does the inner as well as the outer man. He does not leave out important facets of character and personality.

This book, for instance, goes very lightly over the 1930's and 1940's. While I assert that this was, indeed, a period of "somnolence" followed by a period in which World War II almost totally preoccupied Montanans—that is not a sufficiently full explanation. Granted that in the 1930's and 1940's the "uniqueness" of the Montana experience was almost entirely swallowed up by the depression and the war, a complete history would nonetheless contain a balanced review of those years.

The greater problem is that materials for those years have simply not been gathered in sufficient quantity so that generalizations and patterns (beyond those which I *have* dealt with in this book) can be made. The several archives in Montana are quite strong in nineteenth-century Montana, relatively strong up to 1930, and very weak since 1930. Accordingly researchers, with a few exceptions, have steered clear of that period.

Since this is a *generalized* work characterized by a very heavy reliance on master's theses, doctoral dissertations, and articles in obscure journals, the dearth, the paucity, passes itself along the line to the final product—this book.

I do not mean, incidentally, by "a very heavy reliance on master's theses . . ." etc., that I have not gone repeatedly to the sources. I have—either when I was troubled by some illusive aspect of things, or when I was dubious about some aspect of the "secondary" material I was using.

Why then, if one admits to a spotty treatment of the 1930's and 1940's, write a synthesis of Montana in the twentieth century at all? The answer lies in the several considerations: First, there *is* evidence that very few changes of moment in concepts and procedures occurred in those years and that most matters of importance (the state of the economy, the political peregrinations and absurdities, the social milieu) changed very little. Secondly, since almost all writing about Montana history stops at the date of statehood (1889), somewhere along the line someone has to begin, at least, some penetration beyond that date. This book is an attempt, incomplete, to start the process.

In 1965, I began offering a research seminar in Montana history at the University. I had been away from academia for a long time, and I rather dreaded the prospect of somberly presiding over M.A. and Ph.D. candidates as they grubbed their way methodically through the ledgers, letters, diaries, memoirs, old newspapers, and sundry documents that constitute the raw stuff of history in order to produce monumentally dull theses. I agreed with J. Frank Dobie, who had once said, "The average Ph.D. thesis is nothing but the transference of bones from one graveyard to another."

But I found the seminar enormously challenging. It was apparent early in the game that these graduate students were not like those of my day. In the first place, they wanted to work on subjects that threw light on why Montana is what it is today. They exhibited no interest in vigilantes, steamboat days on the Yellowstone River, Indian wars, or gold rushes. Secondly, they were enormously skeptical of me and of each other. And they fell into contentious criticism of each other's work and of mine whenever the tentative product (a research report, a thesis chapter, or an essay) was laid on the line. No reviewer of this book could possibly be as critical of its contents as my own students have been as it has been placed before them in bits and pieces to elicit their comments. On one early draft of what later became Chapter III, "The Boom and the Bust," a student wrote this comment: "Fatuous, sentimental, poorly organized, ineptly written and, withal, not acceptable. See my marginal notes. I suggest you start over—but clear up your thinking first."

With ten to eighteen students a quarter for six years, with most of these students concentrating on the twentieth century and, moreover, digging up other theses and dissertations written at other universities on twentieth-century Montana subjects, it began to dawn on me that a substantial (if very diverse and uneven) body of literature existed on the history of Montana since 1900. Nor was this literature confined to theses and dissertations. Nosing graduate students unearthed articles in obscure journals in economics, journalism, and other disciplines.

One fact emerged in rather short order: a series of events, occurring about the turn of the century, drastically changed the course of the state's development. Although the word "relevance" has been much abused of late, there is no better word to employ in this case. One can never escape a certain abiding continuity in history, but the bulk of what is relevant to today's Montana (and to tomorrow's) developed with crashing suddenness after 1900. The recognition of that fact was the first stimulus for this book. The second was simply that the material which the seminar created, or turned up, ought, somehow, to be tied together into the patterns into which, it seemed to me, it so naturally fell.

Why not, then, an anthology? But, who would publish a ten-volume work? Dozens of theses and dissertations many hundreds of pages long were involved. Some of them were (within themselves) very uneven. And there are a good many recently published books, parts of which, often widely separated, fit into the pattern.

So the answer, partial as it is, is this book. And so, also, Wilson Mizner's definition of research comes into play: "If you steal from one author, it's plagiarism; if you steal from many, it's research." That being, I think, essentially an accurate description for the making of a book like this one, acknowledgments must be more than perfunctory. This would *not* be true if this book were written for the professional historian, for then copious footnotes and detailed citations would indicate with the precision of the appropriate *ibid*s., *op. cit*s., *passim*s, *loc. cit*s., etc., where each bit of information came from. Not only have I grown to abhor these devices in generalized works, I resent them because they invariably inhibit one's own interpretation of other people's recitations of the "facts"; they plunge one into an argument with his sources. I have already argued enough with my own students and have no intention of extending those arguments into this work. However, the bibliographical essay at the end of this book is not merely intended to give the reader a clear idea, chapter by chapter, of where he can pursue various subjects more fully, but is designed specifically to express my debt to some very fine students who have been more than peripherally involved in the creation of this work.

If my treatment of Montana is critical—and it is—it is a criticism that arises from a very strong affection. One tends to feel critical of something one loves, more readily, perhaps, than of something one cares nothing about. States, no less than nations, develop "character," a distinguishing something. They become anthropomorphized; one feels strong loyalties toward them—or antipathies—as if, independent of their transient populations, they had being, something distinct, if residual, lying in the folds of the hills or in the ramparts of the mountains or in the bending grass of the plains.

Montana inspires strong reactions. Writing in the *Partisan Review* in 1948 in an article entitled "The Montana Face," author and critic Leslie Fiedler, then a professor in the University of Montana, had this to say:

> I was met unexpectedly by the Montana face. What I had been expecting I do not clearly know; zest, I suppose; naivete, a ruddy and straightforward kind of vigor—perhaps even honest brutality. What I found seemed, at first glance, reticent, sullen, weary—full of self sufficient stupidity; a little later it appeared simply inarticulate, with all the dumb pathos of what cannot declare itself: a face developed not for sociability or feeling, but for facing into the weather. . . . I felt a kind of innocence behind it, but an innocence difficult to distinguish

from simple ignorance. . . . They [the faces] were conditioned by a mean, a parsimonious culture.

In 1956, Mr. Fiedler had other thoughts about the "Montana Face." In *Montana Opinion* he wrote, "It is vexing to have to say it, but it is only because I like Montana, after all, that I consider it worth raising my voice over its most flagrant weaknesses. . . . There is so much to gripe about, and it is so hard to get anyone to listen; because in the beauty of its natural setting, man, when he is vile (and when is he not?), seems viler than elsewhere."

John Steinbeck, on the other hand, in *Travels With Charley*, had this to say:

> The next passage in my journey is a love affair. I am in love with Montana. For other states I have admiration, respect, recognition, even some affection, but with Montana it is love, and it's difficult to analyze love when you're in it. . . . It seems to me that Montana is a great splash of grandeur. The scale is huge but not overpowering. The land is rich with grass and color, and the mountains are the kind I would create if mountains were ever put on my agenda. Montana seems to me to be what a small boy would think Texas is like from hearing Texans.

In any event, intuition, osmosis, and even perceptive observation are poor substitutes for the recognition that time runs along in its own corridors, doing things to people and places, leaving its residues and cutting its channels. That process is historical.

Like justice blindfolded, the historian is supposed to hold the scales while "the facts" weigh themselves and judgments are rendered accordingly—irrefutable, perforce, and impersonal. It does not work that way, of course, but the thought persists that it should. The mere process of selecting the facts to be weighed involves the historian in the first instance with his point of view and his biases. The best he can do is to involve his integrity and neither hide facts that run contrary to his hypothesis nor unduly favor those that prove his point.

This is a book with a point of view which, hopefully, has been honestly and thoughtfully arrived at, but that is no guarantee that it is the only one or even, for that matter, the right one. However heavily I have leaned on the work of my own students and on others, errors of fact or interpretation are exclusively my own.

K. Ross Toole

TABLE OF CONTENTS

ILLUSTRATIONS

MAPS

TWENTIETH-CENTURY

MONTANA:

A STATE OF EXTREMES

I. THE SETTING

> Countless miracles, boundless prosperity—they would go on and on—it was that simple. . . . By the same token the future was simple. The rewards would go to the virtuous. "A certain manly quality in our people" observed Commentator John Bates Clark, "gives assurance that we have the personal material out of which a millennium will grow."
>
> Walter Lord, *The Good Years*

IF newspapers are a guide to the sentiments of a people (which they frequently are not), there was remarkable unanimity among Montanans as the nineteenth century wheeled in the darkness into the twentieth. There were, to be sure, apologies to be made to the immutable arithmetic of the calendar because everyone knew that the twentieth century began at 12:01, January 1, 1901, rather than 12:01, January 1, 1900, but what mattered was that the 1800's had become the 1900's. The editorial in the *Daily Missoulian* was typical.

> Will those who see the close of the Twentieth Century look back and wonder how the people of this age managed to exist with the crude appliances they had? We think not. There have been some new things but the limit has about been reached in mechanical appliances. . . . It is a reasonable assumption that the world will be a still more desirable place of residence at the close of the Twentieth Century than it is at its beginning.

The average Montanan differed little from the average American; his invincible optimism was matched only by his certitude that the inevitable course of mankind was upward. Indeed, in one retrospective editorial after another, the senti-

3

ment was at least implicit that the pace of progress must surely slow as the perfectible came closer to perfection.

The comfort that America's isolation gave Americans as of 1900 was substantial. If there were a few people who saw dark harbingers in a certain shrinking of the seas, if a few more wondered what American troops were doing in the Philippines, and a few others had seen dangers lurking in the ragged discontent of the farmer and the hot clashes between capital and labor that had characterized the preceding decade, the average American was not concerned. And proceeding inland from the cities, the sense of insulation grew. Nineteen hundred was a good year in America; it was a better year in Montana.

The state was only eleven years old. That it had certain problems no one would deny. They seemed, however, to be exclusively the problems of youth. Insofar as politicians took note of a few developing imbalances in the economy, certain solidifying political postures, and perhaps some inequities among the populace, the solution lay in the absorption of these aberrant tendencies by the continuation of the almost explosive growth of the preceding years. After all, Montana's population had jumped from 39,000 in 1870 to 143,000 in 1890, and to 243,000 by 1900.

The wealth of the area was enormous. In 1899, Montana produced 61 per cent of the copper in the United States and 23 per cent of the production of the world. By 1910 Montana's non-ferrous mines employed 20,000 wage earners who produced $55,000,000 worth of raw wealth. But copper was the cornerstone. Although only thirty-five operators were involved, they employed more than 13,000 people, amounting to about three-fifths of the wage earners of the entire state. In 1909 alone, the copper mines produced $46,000,000 worth of raw wealth. And the giant among them was the Anaconda Copper Mining Company, which was gobbling up competitors with a voracious appetite in the early years of the new century.

By 1910, the Anaconda Company alone owned 1,166,000 acres of timberland. Even that was insignificant. Of the huge state's 93,000,000 acres, more than 22,000,000 were heavily forested. In 1899 Montanans cut, used, or sold more than 255,000 thousand feet of lumber.

The wealth in metal and timber lay in the area west of the Continental Divide, constituting about one-fourth of the entire area of the state. In the east the wealth was largely mobile—cattle and sheep. The state produced more than $4,000,000 worth of wool in 1900, which, by 1910, had jumped to nearly $7,000,000. By the latter year there were more than 490,000 beef cattle on the Montana ranges worth more than $27,000,000.

There were many Montanans who had literally grown up with its cities, and the cities themselves had sprung almost literally from the raw wilderness. A schoolboy in Butte as of 1880, say, when the "camp" had a flotsam-like population of approximately 3,400, could now, in his twenty-fifth year, look out over a boisterous, roaring conglomeration of 30,470 souls. The same schoolboy in 1880 could have hunted deer in the pristine meadows of Nate Levengood's ranch and the only sound he would then have heard was the rustling of the aspen. In 1900 he would find himself on the main street of Anaconda, population 9,800, and towering over him, belching steam and arsenic, and making a racket that shook the countryside, was the largest copper smelter in the world.

Fast as all this had come about, the cities of Montana had an aura of permanence about them. The Victorian mansions

Lewis Wedum drugstore in Glasgow. *Courtesy Montana Historical Society.*

Cattle on their way to market, probably during the period 1895–1905. *Courtesy University of Montana Library.*

Drilling on the 1,900-foot level
of a Butte mine, about 1900.
Courtesy
University
of Montana
Library.

Loading logs with a donkey engine.
Courtesy University of Montana Library.

on Helena's west side already looked as staid as their counterparts on New York's west side; the Broadwater spa six miles to the west, rambling, towered, spacious and plush, was the equal of almost any hostelry in the country. Even in Missoula, the somnolent town west across the Continental Divide, the 4,300 residents took pride in the solidity of the first two buildings that housed the state university. They were new and they looked a little barren, sitting alone as they did on the flat ground south of the town. But they were solid and imposing and there was plenty of room for growth.

However, if there was considerable uniformity in the optimistic view that most Montanans took of their future as of 1900, there were different roots to the sentiment. Western and eastern Montana were profoundly different regions influenced by and dependent upon widely variant resources— weather, soil, and circumstances. The central and eastern portions (comprising about three-quarters of the state) had more in common with each other than either had with the western quarter. Though there were local variations, the area east of the Divide was flat, relatively treeless, semiarid, and its great initial resource was grass. Where irrigation could be employed and the soil was of such composition as to benefit from it, water could, and later did, create oases. But particularly in the eastern section, there were vast areas where water was not available and there were equally large areas through which great rivers passed but in which the soils were simply too poor to sustain farming as such.

The result of these regional differences was a kind of diversity among Montanans that often confused outsiders and that sometimes confused Montanans themselves. It was difficult to generalize about the state's economy or its politics.

In the west, the rivers tumbled out of the mountains with

a kind of turbid profligacy—largely unused. In the east, they moved sluggishly through endless miles of country where, it seemed, they *could* not be used. In the west, the wealth lay bound in the deep rocks of the mountains; in the east, that wealth in the form of bunchgrass and blue grama bent low in the wind. In the mountain valleys of the west, the farmer thought in terms of three or four hundred acres; in the east, the rancher thought in terms of thousands upon thousands of acres.

In the west, the wealth was locked in bedrock, or it grew on the mountain slopes in the form of pine, fir, larch, and spruce that had to be harvested with large crews, heavy equipment, and elaborate planning. In the east, the wealth was mobile—"cattle on a thousand hills" or sheep moving like whitecaps on a sea. These differences conditioned Montanans to ask different things of their government, both local and national, and it conditioned them to react differently to statewide and interstate involvements.

There had been few setbacks in the swift growth of the mining and lumbering enterprises in the west. Prior to 1900, the "War of the Copper Kings" had occupied the political arena, but even when the warring factions carried the conflict, along with their dynamite, underground and into the drifts and stopes of the Butte mines, it had little effect on production. Nor, in spite of a running conflict with the federal government over timber depredations on the public domain that kept Montana's lumbermen in turmoil for eighteen years, was there any interruption in the production of lumber.

But in the eastern section, the growth of the cattle and sheep industries had been sporadic. The terrible winter of 1886–87 had put an end to the open range, and the rancher had had to adjust to barbwire, closed areas, and the winter

15

feeding of his stock. The great herds of sheep that had wandered over ranges as vast as a sea were now, likewise, pushed into narrower confines. Slowly, the ranches were diminishing in size, the farms were getting bigger.

Montana was young not only in political years as of 1900, it was young in the years of its inhabitants. Four and one-third per cent of the national population was over 65—only 2.4 per cent of all Montanans were over 65. More than 19 per cent were between 15 and 24, and there were far more men than women, nearly twice the national figure. Moreover, there was a high percentage of unmarried males—13 per cent higher than the national average.

In the 146,000 square miles that comprised the state, there were only 243,000 Montanans at the turn of the century; only 1.7 persons per square mile. The director of the census in 1890 had defined the "frontier" as an area with less than two persons per square mile—so Montana still qualified. Indeed, even with a decade's swift growth, there were only 2.6 persons per square mile in 1910.

Montanans were aware of their isolation. They could hardly live where they did and not be struck by distance and emptiness. For many of them, the window on the world which the railroads had opened was more apparent than real. Railroads made all the difference to the miners, the lumbermen, and the big merchants and traders, but it remained a fact that the some 3,000 miles of tracks left many others as remote as if the rails had never come at all. If you lived twenty miles from the town (and the track), you lived a long, hard haul away; two days, maybe three.

Haying in the Deer Lodge valley, about 1920. *Courtesy University of Montana Library.*

Pioneer Motor Express at Havre in 1919.
Courtesy Montana Historical Society.

DAYTON, ROLLINS AND SOME

Passenger stage, Dayton, Rollins, and Somers.
Courtesy Montana Historical Society.

In 1900, Montana had less than 15,000 miles of so-called "public roads." But traffic on these "arteries" was seasonal, to say the least. Even by 1910, when the figure had jumped to 23,000 miles, the fact remained that that meant only .16 miles of road per square mile of Montana.

Butte was the only city in the state with a population of more than 25,000. There were only ten places with populations in excess of 2,500, six of which were less than 5,000. There were sixteen with less than 2,500. Some 143,000 Montanans, in other words, lived in no town at all—nearly 60 per cent of the population.

Montana's largest telephone company had only 1,300 miles of line by 1902. The telephone was still a curiosity; there were only some 5,000 telephone sets in use, and "use" was more an adventure than a reliable means of communication.

Most Montanans, in other words, lived a long way from most other Montanans and a longer way still from the east–west axis of trade. If their isolation from each other was marked, their isolation from "any place else," especially in the long winter months, was almost complete.

So, often and perforce, Montanans turned inward. Isolation also meant insulation. Especially in the east, they gathered when they could to exchange what they could, and in a sense they waited. Sometimes, east and west, they cursed the distance and the space because they knew what it cost—or thought they did.

Why, then, the optimism, the ebullience, the youthful exuberance? Because it was all here, waiting—the enormous wealth, the limitless land, the great rivers, the thousand things that spoke of the future. And it was all very new—waiting.

It would have been a rare Montanan in the year 1900 who really believed that the wait might be a long one. And it would have been a rarer Montanan, still, who would have doubted that when it all came, it would be a blessing unmixed.

II. IT IS STILL NOT
TOO LATE—GO WEST

Honyocker, scissorbill, nester. . . . He was the Joad of a quarter century ago, swarming into a hostile land; duped when he started, robbed when he arrived; hopeful, courageous, ambitious; he sought independence or adventure, comfort and security. . . . Hurry, honyocker, and do not investigate too closely.

J. K. Howard, *Montana: High, Wide, and Handsome*

THE U.S. census is a remarkable compilation of facts, figures, measurements, quantities, and statistics. Revealing as it is, it is not really the record of a people. It is a snapshot taken every ten years, freezing for that instant into figures, graphs, and charts certain postures of America. But in the years between, things come and go, rise and fall, appear and disappear and are never noted in the census at all. That is one of the reasons the honyocker[1] is so hard to come to grips with. Between 1910 and 1920 a horde of homesteaders poured into the northern Great Plains. They came from diverse places for a variety of reasons and yet, in a deeper sense, they had the same reasons, listened to the same drummer.

At the time of the census of 1910, the plains had yet to feel their impact; before the census taker made his rounds in 1920, most of them had left. Reading between the lines and piecing things together from other sources, one gets a glimpse

---

[1] The origin of the word honyocker is obscure. It was apparently an offshoot of the word Hunyak, meaning an immigrant from Central Europe. It was a term of derision applied to all "outlanders."

25

of the ruin they left behind them—vacant towns, sagging grain elevators, roads that led nowhere, and tumbleweeds scudding on the edge of a hot wind.

If the honyocker was himself wounded by the failure that caused his exodus, the land he left behind was wounded also —and it recovered more slowly than he did. Turn the face of native grass downward with the plow and more dies than the grass; the land itself dies—it blows away.

It is estimated that between 70,000 and 80,000 people flooded into eastern and central Montana between 1909 and 1918 and that at least 60,000 left before 1922. But that is an estimate. No one really knows, and the census is essentially mute. When the drought came and the bewildered honyocker had left, J. L. Humphrey, a Montana banker, expressed the prevailing view of the situation: "History shows that the first settlers in any country are never good farmers. . . . A new country has never made any progress until the second or third sets of land owners have moved in."

Was it, then, the honyocker himself who brought about the catastrophe? Many Montanans thought so. After all, said the state Commissioner of Agriculture, "There were men induced to enter farming who had no previous experience, such as clerks, barbers, factory hands and others." Writing bitterly some years later, Joseph Kinsey Howard noted, "Thus the comfortable conviction took root that the honyockers, a stupid lot, had only themselves to blame."

Yet, if they were poor farmers, or if some of them were merely speculators, the fact remains that they worked unremittingly and effectively in the face of odds more appalling than those faced on most earlier frontiers.

In 1909, only 250,000 acres were planted in wheat in Montana; by 1919, this had risen to 35,000,000 acres. In just over ten years the honyocker had taken up over 40 per cent of the entire area of the state. He had founded dozens of raw, ugly, and utilitarian towns; he had built roads, bridges, schools, and churches; and he had produced wheat: 3,560 thousands of bushels in 1909, 40,852 thousands of bushels by 1924.

Yet it *is* true that a disproportionate number of honyockers had never farmed before. A subsequent study made in the north-central district of Montana indicated that 51 per cent of the settlers had had no previous farming background. Seventy per cent of those who had settled without previous agricultural experience failed and left the land, while only 48 per cent of those with a farming background abandoned their farms. While the study purported to demonstrate that farming experience was short among the honyockers and that that shortage of experience was critical in the events that occurred, the compelling fact is that even among the experienced nearly half failed and moved on.

If the honyocker was ignorant of the physiographic limitations of the area (with which ignorance he was subsequently often indicted) so, largely, were the agricultural scientists. They knew far too little to give sound advice. They had few precipitation records, knew even less about evaporation rates and practically nothing about soils.

The subsequent assumption by many Montanans that the honyocker fell victim to outside exploiters and external agencies (primarily land companies and railroads) who callously used the naïve settler for private profit is largely untrue. The old-time rancher, the state Bureau of Labor, Agriculture, and Industry, the local banker, the merchant, chambers of commerce, and real estate dealers aggressively and enthusiastically participated in a promotional campaign of great

27

Breaking sod in the good days before the drought, East Coleridge community, about 1909. *Photograph by N. B. Seiverud, courtesy Montana Historical Society.*

magnitude. If their previous tenure in the area *had* made them knowledgeable, it was not evident. Perhaps it is more charitable to conclude that they did not know the land themselves —or that they came to believe their own propaganda.

The honyocker is hard to deal with, also, because the region he inhabited was varied. Western North and South Dakota were involved, along with the eastern two-thirds of Montana. But the movement was wider than that and even in this northern Great Plains region the settlers' experiences were far from identical. When the drought that marked their nemesis came, it did not come to all of the region at once; it was not consistent in its tenacity everywhere and all the time, nor did all the honyockers settle in the plains region. Some passed it by and settled in the mountain valleys. Some, with luck and grim determination, weathered the drought on the plains and stayed put. We do not know what percentage made it; we do know that it was small.

Why did they come when they came and in such numbers? The answer lies in a strange kind of fortuity, a combination of circumstances that fell almost at random into a pattern of tragedy.

The flood of settlers might never have come (at least as a flood) if the pieces of the pattern, some very old, some new, had not fallen into place to create, quite suddenly, a picture of bright but illusory promise. Behind it and fundamental to it lay a hunger for land, free land, whetted by a federal government that had long since committed itself to the disposal of the vast public domain—free of charge.

In 1905, the government's policy notwithstanding, more

Crossing Peeks Coulee on way to Sour Dough, 1909. *James Fergus Collection, courtesy University of Montana Library.*

than 56,000,000 acres of the public domain were unreserved and unoccupied in the northern plains region. Of these acres, 41,043,000 were in Montana east of the mountains.

The law that basically governed the disposal of public lands at this time was the much honored and much misunderstood Homestead Act of 1862. It had been amended many times by 1905, but it still provided that a settler might acquire 160 acres for a nominal filing fee provided he resided continually on it and cultivated it for five years. If the settler chose, he could commute his claim—that is, by paying $1.25 per acre, he could gain title after fourteen months of residence.

There was another option under the Desert Land Act of 1877 by virtue of which a homesteader could obtain 320 acres of land by making nominal payments per acre, but he was required to irrigate and cultivate one-eighth of his tract.

The principle of small homestead settlement was deeply imbedded in federal policy and in Congressional attitudes and philosophy. It was a humid-area concept that fit nicely with the determination to prevent the amassing of large holdings by a small number of individuals. While Westerners, and many Easterners as well, knew that such limited acreage on the semiarid plains was wholly uneconomic and discouraged settlement, they believed that the answer lay not in expanded acreage, but in irrigation. They had a common fear of speculators and great "empires" in private hands. Indeed, no one in the Congress was more insistent on small-unit disposal of public lands than Montana's own Senator Paris Gibson, who even proposed a bill calling for repeal of the Desert Land Act and the commutation clause of the original Homestead Act. Gibson's effort met some opposition in Montana, but it was neither concerted nor widespread. Behind this emphasis on small acreage (which was rapidly breaking down in the West by 1905) lay an old misconception regarding irrigation on the plains. What the Nile could do for the Egyptian desert, the great Western rivers could surely do for the "Great American Desert."

The early reclamationists were dreamers. Their fancies involved reclamation via dams, ditches, ponds, and diversions. The idea that the semiarid and arid midriff of the country needed only water (and water, they said, could readily be diverted from its network of great rivers) died slowly. It was an idea deeply seated in early "scientific" reports and even more deeply rooted in the experiences of humid-area agriculturalists.

The prestigious John Wesley Powell, the father of reclamation, once reported to Congress that in due course a fish culture would replace a cattle culture on the Great Plains. Although Powell himself later came to realize that aridity was the nature of the plains and that even the great network of rivers could not slake the thirst, others less inclined to test and study continued to recommend massive federal irrigation projects to make the desert bloom.

Indeed, these early reclamationists had an argument that appeared sound simply because of the hundreds of billions of gallons of water that poured down daily from the Rocky Mountains and flowed, unused, across the dry plains. A glance at a map (with the great arteries emphasized) was enough to prove the point. Reclamation became an article of faith leading ultimately to heavy federal involvement.

While there were some protests, and while scientific studies initiated by Powell and others increasingly gave the lie to the claims of the zealots, the creation of a lush garden from the burned midsection of the country had caught the public fancy —and the fancy of Congress.

33

One Montanan told a U.S. Senate committee in 1889, that when spread over the dry soil of Montana, water produced Kentucky bluegrass within a season; General John Gibbon testified, presumably on the basis of study and experience, that canals in Montana could replace railroads for the transportation of logs to the lumber mills in the west. There was much interest in canals for more varied transportation needs on the plains proper.

Every farm was to have its pond and not only would fish supplant beef, but pond vegetation could be harvested and used for fertilizer. What is more, with the creation of a garden in mid-America, the hot winds would no longer blow across the face of Kansas, but would become moist zephyrs, saturated with the evaporated water of the plains to the west. These and dozens of other plans and views set forth by presumably expert people, led the Congress inexorably to its involvement in reclamation.

The reclamation projects failed—at least in the sense that no garden came forth and irrigation proved something less than a panacea. In Montana, projects got underway slowly; they involved high costs and very limited acreage. Few farmers could afford the $20- to $60-per-acre cost to participate. The result, even though projects were launched on the Milk River, the Sun River, on the lower Yellowstone, and at Huntley (east of Billings), was a growing disillusionment with reclamation—and this disillusionment extended to all of the West.

The preoccupation with irrigation had obscured the fact that for twenty-five years dry-land farming had been conducted successfully in regions where the rainfall, though marginal, was sufficient. Dry farming, or dry-land farming, was nothing new in the United States. Defined as the practice of agriculture without irrigation in semiarid regions, it had been extensively practiced in western Kansas and Nebraska in the 1880's.

When it became obvious that reclamation was not the answer, interest turned to "scientific" dry-land farming and a new crop of zealots entered the picture. They, too, turned their attention to the Great Plains; they, too, began to talk of "the great garden"; they, too, devised plans as bizarre as they were absurd. They were joined, ultimately, by railroad magnates, by chambers of commerce, by organizations specifically devised to pressure the Congress, and by state legislatures in the semiarid states.

The ultimate result was the passage of the Enlarged Homestead Act of 1909. The legislation passed in spite of a National Conservation Commission's strong recommendation that prior to any change in land laws, the nation's remaining public domain be "classified." Scientific classification, said the Commission's report, "would ultimately fix with certainty, according to the productive value of the surface, a reasonable home-making area for each class of agricultural land, and thus solve that problem without mistake or friction."

By the time of the Commission's report (February, 1909), the pressure for a liberalized land law had become overwhelming. Reclamation was "out"; dry-land farming was "in"; the law passed handily.

One of the powerful proponents of the act of 1909 was Montana's Senator Joseph M. Dixon. The original proposal as set forth by Dixon called for 640 acres. In the debate that ensued it was, strangely enough, the Eastern and Middle-Western opponents of the proposal who made the most sense.

"If," said Congressman Paul Howland of Ohio, "he [the homesteader] cannot make a living on 160 acres of land,

35

Grain wagons at Big Sandy in 1916.
Courtesy Montana Historical Society.

there is something the matter with the homesteader or the land. If the trouble is with the land, a greater quantity of that will not help the situation."

William A. Reeder of Kansas, no stranger to dry land, said, "the bill will have the effect of getting people to live on the land . . . but the settler cannot make a living on 640 acres or even 1,280 acres . . . there is the trouble."

Yet the Westerners also had considerable Eastern support. Congressman Rainey of Illinois expressed concern that "fifty to one hundred thousand farmers each year are crossing our northern boundary to settle upon the wheat lands of Canada. . . . A man cannot make a living on 160 acres of non-irrigable land; but if you give him 320 acres, ultimately he will farm half of it one year and half of it the next year under the new system of dry farming. . . ."

Dixon's proposal for 640 acres lost, but the compromise bill of 320 acres passed on February 19, 1909. It required the settler to cultivate at least one-eighth of his acreage beginning with the second year and at least a quarter section by the third year, but all that really mattered was that the homesteader could now get 320 acres of free land.

In 1912, the so-called Three-Year Homestead Act offered added inducement. It reduced the "prove-up" time of five years to three years and allowed the homesteader to be absent from his claim for five months of the year. It reduced the cultivation requirements of the act of 1909 by one-half and allowed the homesteader to commute his claim after only fourteen months of residence.

The laws of 1909 and 1912 were liberalizations, but they were hardly revolutionary. What mattered is that they constituted significant added enticement to an already enticing set of circumstances.

Since shortly after the turn of the century an accelerating promotional campaign aimed at attracting settlers to the northern plains had been underway. It had been initiated by the railroads, whose passage across the barren and unproductive midriff of the country was mileage without profit. Their initial efforts were quickly joined by Midwestern land speculators. The West, even in the light of tourist promotion a half century later, has never seen the like of the campaign. Topped off by the passage of the Enlarged Homestead Act, the roots of the movement are traceable to a dry-land farmer named Hardy Webster Campbell.

At least it may be said of Campbell that he did not bring to the semiarid regions (as was usually the case) a system and philosophy nurtured in the humid areas. He was born in Vermont in 1850, left home at sixteen, worked his way slowly westward doing odd jobs, and finally settled in 1879 on a homestead in Brown County, Dakota Territory.

He was observant and curious and what later came to be called the "Campbell System" began to emerge in his mind when he noted that grass grew thick and green in horse tracks and wheel ruts where the soil had been compacted, while everywhere else his land lay baking in the Dakota sun.

Campbell instructed a local blacksmith to build a soil compacter to his precise specifications. It consisted of a series of wedge-shaped tampers revolving on an axle. The tampers were shaped so as to loosen the topsoil for mulch while packing the subsoil tightly. This was the basic method upon which he elaborated the ultimate "Campbell System." His soil tamper and evolving ideas attracted little attention among his neighbors, but they did interest the Northern Pacific Railroad.

By 1895, Campbell was operating five farms for the Northern Pacific in North Dakota, and under railroad auspices was

39

delivering lectures to farm groups over a wide area. Soon his services were sought by the Burlington and the Chicago and Northwestern, and he became the supervisor of various railroad-owned experimental farms.

In 1895, Campbell began to expound his views in *The Western Soil Culture*, a magazine that he launched with railroad support. By this time, the "Campbell System" was beginning to emerge. Added to subsurface packing was deep plowing, frequent cultivation of the surface, seeding grain in rows so that cultivation could take place between rows, especially early in the season. Later he was to add what he called "summer culture," which was, in effect, summer fallow. By 1902, the system was rounded out with specific instructions for seeding, weeding, discing, and harrowing. Even the diameter of the discs was specified. In 1902, also, Campbell produced the first copy of the *Soil Culture Manual*, which became an annual publication.

Campbell's entire interest lay in preparation of the seed bed and not in the grain seed itself. He had no interest in whether a grain was suited to the semiarid region or not. His system, he said, was applicable to wheat and corn but was just as effective for vegetables or any other crop, including alfalfa. He did not believe in crop rotation or diversification. He was messianic in his conviction that his system resulted in complete control by the farmer of the moisture in the soil, totally precluding crop failure due to drought. Climactic conditions, he said, meant nothing. Rain, as a matter of fact, leached the fertility out of the soil. Thus the soil in semiarid regions was much more fertile than in humid regions. Accordingly, a farmer in semiarid country "can grow better average crops than they are growing in Illinois today, because we can secure the ideal condition, and control it, and they cannot do it in Illinois because they have too much rain."

Between 1902 and 1914, Campbell's influence spread widely throughout the nation. In 1906 an association was formed in Denver called the Campbell System Farming Association of Denver, Colorado. This organization evolved into the Dry Farming Congress, which met annually in a different plains city. By 1910 the Congress had 10,500 dues-paying members. The meeting at Lethbridge, Canada, in 1911 attracted 10,000 people to its sessions.

Moreover, Campbell and the Campbell system were attracting national attention through articles in *The American Review of Reviews*, *Century*, *The World Today*, *The Nation*, and *World's Work*. A story on Campbell in 1912, by A. P. Hitchcock in *Country Life*, for instance, was entitled "The Farmer Who Found Another Half of the World."

The most notable thing about the Dry Farming Congress was the paucity of actual farmers in attendance. It was, in fact, avowedly a propaganda organization, heavily subsidized by the railroads, bankers, chambers of commerce, state publicity departments, and real estate brokers.

Even so, Campbell and the Campbell system did not go unchallenged in the congress, or, for that matter, by agronomists and trained agriculturalists elsewhere. But they were few. E. C. Chilcott, a former agronomist at the South Dakota Agricultural Experiment Station, wrote in 1903, "They [Campbell's supporters] hold out hopes that are never realized and often induce people who can ill afford it to go to considerable expense in adopting a system that will not work in practice," and, in a prophetic warning he concluded, "No method of tillage can entirely overcome the effects of the serious shortage of rainfall which has in the past and probably will in the future, be experienced in the Great Plains area."

Montana's leading agricultural newspaper, *The Rocky Mountain Husbandman*, brilliantly edited by R. N. Sutherlin, conducted a sustained editorial attack on the false claims of the promoters and on Campbell. "Dry farming," wrote Sutherlin, "is a misleading misnomer and it misrepresents our conditions here to the easterner or would-be settler." Central and eastern Montana were dry, said Sutherlin, and *no* system could prevent catastrophe when the inevitable cycle came. Some sections would receive less than two inches of rainfall— and that at the wrong time. That, said Sutherlin, represented disaster to the man foolish enough to believe the propaganda.

But other Montana newspapers reflected the prevailing view of Campbell's system. *The Great Falls Tribune* said, "Hardy Webster Campbell, the father of dry land farming, has brought a miracle to the plains states. Now half of their area can be reclaimed without irrigation and they will be the last and best garden of the world." The *Havre Plaindealer* said: "Campbell's soil culture method provides farmers with enough security to laugh at the severest drouth ever known to them." The *Husbandman* was a small still voice.

When the Dry Farming Congress met in Billings in 1909, even the Department of Agriculture in the person of Lyman J. Briggs had grown cautious. In spite of the splendid activities of the congress, said Briggs, different methods had to be adopted for different localities and circumstances, and no all-inclusive system was practicable.

But the congress was controlled by the promoters, not by farmers or trained agriculturalists. The Billings assembly in 1909 was addressed by Howard Elliot, president of the Northern Pacific Railroad, who said: "We know Montana is neither dry or [*sic*] arid, and we do not want that idea to go down to Indiana and Ohio and through the East where they are looking for new places to go." Lewis W. Hill, president of the Great Northern, was more vehement. ". . . it is desirable to start with a good impression, and do not give the people whom you expect to come here an impression that they are going to a dry country. . . . Montana is neither arid nor dry."

The congress had enormous influence in attracting settlers to the semiarid regions. The meetings were covered by the Associated Press and representatives of the large Midwestern newspapers. The fact that in its bulletins and other publications it often disseminated sound agricultural information was far outweighed by the general impression its propaganda created in the minds of those who were to become the honyockers. From 1907 to 1915, from coast to coast and even abroad, the congress trumpeted the virtues of dry-land farming. It did so with skill and persistence, and the small internal voices of dissent were seldom heard. The smallest voice of all was that of the farmer himself, the man struggling with the land. As Governor Byrn of South Dakota noted at the meeting in 1915, "The real farmer is not here." And, indeed, he was not and never had been. He was too busy struggling with the sun-baked earth, watching the deep skies of May and June for cumulus clouds, and wondering if the bank would once again extend his note.

Although Campbell and the congress were enormously influential, the railroads did not confine themselves to endorsing Campbell and supporting the organization. Indeed, after 1912 they turned increasingly elsewhere.

The Great Northern and the Northern Pacific hired their own "expert" in Montana, Professor Thomas Shaw. Less dogmatic than Campbell, Shaw also commanded respect because he had been a professor (of animal husbandry) at the Minnesota Agricultural College.

The homestead of August and Sabin Berg at Willard.
Courtesy Montana Historical Society.

Homesteader freighting household goods in East Coleridge
community. *Photograph by N. B. Seiverud, courtesy Montana Historical Society.*

By 1910, Shaw was managing forty-five experimental farms for the Great Northern in Montana; he was writing tracts on dry-land farming that received wide distribution through railroad outlets. He spoke to groups in the Midwest and on the West Coast—always with vast enthusiasm for the future of dry-land farming in Montana—and he dispensed advice liberally. He was less rigid than Campbell, but he always included the recommendation, "plow deep." If his advice was broader, if he occasionally recommended a measure of the diversification that Campbell scorned, like Campbell he advocated an emphasis on tillage practices that were enormously dangerous in a semiarid region.

The railroads extended their campaigns even farther. They opened display booths in St. Paul; they ran demonstration trains filled with farm products from the plains area. They established special rates for the honyocker. The Northern Pacific had a special rate of $22.50 from St. Paul, $30 from St. Louis, and $27.50 from Minneapolis to Billings. Or, the honyocker could rent his own freight car for $50 in which he could carry stipulated articles including animals, lumber, fence posts, and household goods. C. W. Mott, immigration agent for the Northern Pacific, approached Montanans for advertising material. He said: "An education war will be made in the respective states that our railroad traverses, and Montana must be sufficiently patriotic to furnish enough literature. . . ." Montana did. It was the largest advertising campaign the railroad had ever undertaken.

The Milwaukee guaranteed that it would place literature describing the advantages of Montana in the hands of 30,000 Eastern farmers—and it did so. As did the other lines, it painted a glowing picture. In a pamphlet on Fergus County distributed by the Milwaukee it claimed that a twenty-bushel-per-acre yield in the Judith Basin was small. The average yield was 40 to 60 bushels! In the *Great Northern Bulletin*, eastern Montana farm lands were described as "the best in the United States; 320 acre homesteads are slipping away so rapidly that a young man back east had better wake up before his birthright slips away. . . ."

Although it has been fashionable to blame the railroads for exploiting the ignorant and naïve, they were, in fact, more forthright and less prone to superlatives than were Montana's chambers of commerce and its state Bureau of Labor, Agriculture, and Industry. Commercial clubs and special promotional organizations sprang up in nearly every eastern and central Montana community. Literature printed and distributed by these organizations presented grossly inaccurate figures and statistics. They misrepresented rainfall, soil, temperatures, and the cost of living. This literature was distributed not only on exhibition trains, but through real estate agents, especially in the Midwest. One piece of literature produced by the Yellowstone National Land Company concerning land it held in the Madison Valley was so grossly inaccurate that Governor Edwin L. Norris called it "a fake of the first order" and asked the citizens of Madison County to counteract it with a pamphlet which would not mislead the interested "investors."

There *was* cynicism. C. W. Mott of the Northern Pacific was delighted with a booklet produced by the state Bureau of Labor, Agriculture, and Industry because, he said, "this book had more weight than almost any kind of publicity . . . because land companies and railroad companies have personal intentions; a book under the hand and seal of Montana is looked upon as an honest and accurate description of the country . . . often when we send printed matter to homeseekers, we follow with the state book so that the recipient believes he has been contacted by state authorities."

The state itself was soon deeply involved in the campaign through its Bureau of Labor, Agriculture, and Industry and through the statewide Montana Development League. Cities, counties, and dozens of regional promotional organizations all joined the railroads in concerted and sustained promotional activity. The jaundiced editor of the *Rocky Mountain Husbandman* remarked, ". . . if a man is going to try dry farming, he must farm on a large acreage, and those who attempt it on a small scale will fail . . . there are good years, but in the bad years, yields only run from 4 to 6 bushels per acre." But no one listened.

The real estate brokers moved in from both East and West. William H. Brown, one of the largest "colonizers" in the country bought extensive acreage in the Lewistown-Utica area. Brown was from Chicago. The Adams brothers, from the same city, bought 50,000 acres in the Musselshell Valley. Brown shortly joined the Adamses in setting up an immigration bureau to attract settlers to their holdings in the Judith Basin area. C. S. Jones, a banker and real estate broker from Walla Walla, Washington, bought extensive tracts of land in Fergus County. "Outlanders" began to appear in most of the towns of eastern and central Montana. Hotel facilities were severely strained.

Nor were all the real estate dealers from out of state. The Hilger Loan and Realty Company of Lewistown was active in purchasing land for resale to settlers. New realty companies sprouted all over the region in Lewistown, Vandalia, Malta, Billings, Culbertson, Great Falls, and even Two Dot.

The "classic" conflict between the cattleman and the homesteader did not occur in Montana—or at least it was rare.

Indeed, the ranchers participated with a vengeance. Joseph A. Baker, a stockman from Highwood, spoke for a good many ranchers when he said, "Dry farming is the coming salvation of the west . . . I plan to put the dry farming system into effect on my Highwood land which has heretofore been considered by men as nothing but poor grazing land."

In the Musselshell Valley two ranches of 40,000 and 26,000 acres each were sold to real estate dealers, and the *Musselshell News* concluded that the available acreage was sufficient "for twenty-five families to settle on." Ranchers, at least, were aware that 160 to 320 acres of dry land could not sustain a family.

Two additional circumstances fell into place just at the right time to complete the picture of the garden. From 1910 to 1917 it rained—an annual average of 16 inches—and at the right time, in May and June. Between 1900 and 1916 eastern and central Montana produced an annual average of more than twenty-five bushels of wheat to the cultivated acre. The crop reports filtered and then flooded back to the Midwest and to the East.

Particularly in the Midwest, land prices had skyrocketed. Between 1900 and 1910 the average value of farm land in the United States had increased from $20 to $40 per acre. In Kansas during the same decade, farm land value increased 157 per cent and in Nebraska, 177 per cent. In Montana, with luck, a man could file on 320 acres and buy an equal amount for $10 to $20 per acre. And even if he couldn't farm that much, land was appreciating rapidly. One could make money simply by waiting.

Then there was the last circumstance that drew the honyocker to the semiarid lands. The war. America was the bread basket of Europe; the new Federal Reserve Board in

Stage between Great Falls and Lewistown, about 1909. This 120-mile trip took fifteen hours. *Courtesy Montana Historical Society.*

Steam-powered farm tractor, date unknown.
Courtesy Montana Historical Society.

Thrashing near Bozeman, about 1910. *Courtesy University of Montana Library.*

Washington had so loosened the reins of credit that almost anyone could get an agricultural loan. A National Council of Defense which, in turn, had spawned forty-eight state councils of defense, joined in urging non-farmers to farm and those who were already farming to expand—and the emphasis was on wheat. By 1916 wheat was selling for $1.43 per bushel; by 1917 it had jumped to $2.04. America's actual entry into the war led to talk of $4.00-a-bushel wheat.

All factors put together, the infallible "Campbell System," the homestead acts of 1909 and 1912, the great promotional campaigns of the railroads, the land companies and the governments of the states involved, the "accident" of wet years between 1909 and 1917, the easy credit, the high price of land elsewhere, and the war-induced skyrocketing price of wheat—all these mingled in the voice of the siren that beckoned the honyocker westward.

And so they came—in sleepers, freight cars, model T's, old trucks. They came to Culbertson, Ekalaka, Harlowton, Billings, and Ubet; they climbed stiffly down onto station platforms in the flat glare of the sun and looked out over a country of endless sameness—immense, flat, and formidable. A nameless honyocker who arrived thus at Dutton asked the station master where he could find a "locator." The weary railroader sighed and looked up, "Just go down the street and look like a sucker and George Sollid will find you."

III. THE BOOM
AND THE BUST

> But the lesson that the plains settler could not
> learn, short of living it out, was that no system of
> farming, no matter how strenuously applied, could
> produce crops in that country during one of the
> irregular and unpredictable periods of drought and
> that the consequences of trying to force the issue
> could be disastrous to both people and land.

Wallace Stegner, *Wolf Willow*

I

BETWEEN 1900 and 1910, dry-land farm values doubled in the foothill section of Montana, tripled in the triangle area of the north, and quadrupled in the Judith Basin area. Land companies by the latter year were doing a frenetic business. By 1918 land was selling at such a high price that L. C. Gray of the Department of Agriculture felt compelled to warn that at such prices, loose credit notwithstanding, a farmer had little chance of making a success of his venture.

In 1908, the *Wibaux Pioneer* noted with awe that homestead filings had reached some sixteen a week for the general area. But within a year, entries at the Miles City Land Office were coming in at the rate of 1,200 a month.

On one day alone in 1910, 250 honyockers arrived in Havre; the Great Falls office was processing 1,000 to 1,500 entries per month. The Great Northern reported 1,100 carloads of emigrant materials hauled into eastern Montana between January 1 and April 15, 1910. By 1913, the Havre Land Office was handling 700 filings per month.

None of these records, of course, include homesteaders who were buying private land. Northern Pacific Railway lands were selling at a rate that made the processing of sales almost impossible. In 1916 alone the railroad sold 1,313,472 acres in Montana.

Still they came. In 1916 there were 1,200 new arrivals during the single month of March in Havre. Wolf Point, Geraldine, Roy, Winnifred, Grass Range, Box Elder, Big Sandy, and Conrad were all jammed with arriving homesteaders. The "locators" were working from dawn to dusk. The land offices were swamped.

Incomplete as census figures are, they give some idea of the magnitude of the flood. Between 1900 and 1920, the population of Montana as a whole rose from just under a quarter of a million to just over half a million, but the plains counties alone increased by more than 220,000 persons

A freighting outfit belonging to Joe Hartmann. *Courtesy Montana Historical Society.*

—and these figures were rendered in 1920 when the exodus had already well begun! The actual number of farms in existence in the eastern counties rose from 7,000 in 1900 to 46,000 in 1920.

Whatever his hardships, however grim the heat, however faceless the country, the honyocker had his hope to go on. If he had made money on any given crop, he had used it as a down payment for more land or equipment. He rarely had money in the bank or cash in his pocket. He spent little, if anything, on his house or comforts, and his living standard was elemental.

He lived, probably, twenty miles or more from the nearest town and, particularly in the early period, as far or farther from his nearest neighbor. His house was perhaps twelve by eighteen feet, two rooms, one outside door, and perhaps two

The Eversons' sod house near Big Sandy in the spring of 1914. *Photograph by Alta Deem, courtesy Montana Historical Society.*

windows. His insulation was tar paper or, in many cases, newspapers glued to the wall with flour-and-water paste.

One study estimated the cost of such a dwelling at about $100. The stable, shed, and hen house, similarly constructed, cost another several hundred. What the honyocker had to have was land, and the animals or machinery to work it. His capital, grossly limited in any event, did not go for comforts. He was a bad carpenter and often used green lumber hauled from the railroad. He had no paint, so his house and outbuildings shriveled in the sun and warped and cracked. The tar paper blew off in the howling wind and he stuffed rags in the holes.

In the wintertime, the cast-iron stove, stuffed to the top with twisted bunches of grass and chips of wood (rarely with chunks of coal that had to be hauled from the railroad), turned red-hot but warmed only its immediate vicinity, while a blue-white circle of frost encompassed the rest of the house. The family slept, when they slept at all, around the stove, while a universe of hostile frigidity and moaning wind surrounded them just beyond the guttering light from the kerosene lamp. In the incredibly bitter and long winters of the plains it was not unusual for the honyocker to burn first his fence posts, if he had any, and then his sheds to keep his family from freezing.

Water was a constant problem. Underground water was either too deep for practical drilling, or, if present and near enough to the surface, was so brackish as to be unpotable. The honyocker either hauled his water in barrels from the railroad, or employed cisterns or shallow reservoirs. Windmills were rare because of the depth of the water and the expense of drilling. The "epizootic," diarrhea, various stomach disorders, and typhoid were common.

The settler could rarely fence his acreage. In 1910 it cost $160 for the materials to fence 320 acres; by 1915 this had risen to $220. Crop losses due to roaming livestock were often heavy. Montana's herd laws were designed by ranchers, and the honyocker had no legal recourse.

A large percentage of the men went off during the winter to work for the railroad or the granary in the nearest town, leaving the wives to fend for themselves. Often the frequent blizzards prevented the man from returning on weekends and for days on end, the wife and the children huddled in the shack, board by board burning the homestead to stay alive.

Especially in the early period, domestic animals, unused to fending for themselves in a country which even the buffalo had deserted in deep winter, weakened, starved, and died.

From 1909 to 1917, they stayed. When the spring came they planted, they sweated and baked throughout the summer, but when the fall came they harvested. They hauled the wheat to the town and the granary in grain-box wagons, 125 bushels to the wagon. A good man could load five or six a day.

In spite of the great distances between farms, they helped each other with the harvest—and when it was over they gathered in the town—wives, kids and clean overalls—where there was little to do but talk or shop for staples. It was a rare honyocker who drank or gambled. These towns were not created for diversion but for cold, hard utility—granary, general store, bank, and church; hot, dusty, flat, and gray. The railroad tracks stretched off in a straight line forever— and the honyocker rode home that October day across the dry, russet land to start it all over again. He may, indeed, not have been the farmer he should have been, but given hope and promise he was as tough and tenacious a human being as ever occupied a frontier.

Pioneering honyockers. *Photograph by Ralph D. Paine,* Outing Magazine, *April, 1906, courtesy Montana Historical Society.*

Russell-Miller Company flour mill in Sidney, 1925.
Courtesy University of Montana Library.

II

It started in the spring of 1917—not everywhere, not all at once. At first it was spotty and confined to the northern counties. Havre, center of much honyocker activity, reported only 0.33 of an inch of rain in May and June and only 0.45 of an inch in July. That meant a near total loss—not a poor crop, but grain burned to the roots. The humidity hovered near 4 per cent. Heat waves shimmered up from a baking, cracking earth. Old stubble had turned from yellow to deep brown by mid-June and had crumbled into black dust by mid-July. The *Havre Plaindealer* called the drought "the worst in the history of the state."

There were hotly glowing spots of drought in central and eastern Montana, like metastasized cells of a cancer. Then the grasshoppers came in dark sky-waves, clacking, fluttering, and gushing. They settled on everything like an obscene blanket. The *Wibaux Pioneer* recommended a poisoned bran-mash concentration broadcast from a wagon or buggy, but the hoppers devoured the poison and clacked on. Wireworm and cutworm were worse than the hoppers. "Experts" recommended a solution of arsenic sprinkled on chopped fruit, but where was the honyocker to get chopped fruit? Sometimes he simply broadcast the arsenic, sometimes he made a mash of arsenic and paper or sawdust, but the worms were unaffected.

That first year the heart of the drought was in the north—Teton, Pondera, Hill, Blaine, Phillips, Valley, and Sheridan counties. In Hill County the honyockers harvested but two bushels to the acre in the fall of 1917; Blaine County farmers realized only half a bushel per acre. Central and eastern Montana were as yet affected only in isolated spots. The yield in Cascade County was 30 bushels; in the Judith Basin, 15 bushels.

The initial reaction to the trouble in the north was philosophical. The Fergus County *Argus* blamed the low yield on careless farming; there was little statewide concern. The honyocker in the north tightened his belt, battened down for the long winter, plowed deep, and borrowed the money for his seed. The banks carried him.

The spring came early, hot and dry—and now the utterly clear, thin sky extended over central and eastern Montana. On June 14, 1918, the *Havre Plaindealer* reported that Richland and Musselshell counties were being swept by hot, dry winds. In Yellowstone, Rosebud, and Carter counties the crop had been burned out by mid-June. Carter County is in the extreme southeast corner of the state.

The summer and fall of 1918 were unrelievedly grim. The winds spread; they swept across the entire area with maddening strength and constancy. They tattered the tar paper on the honyocker's shack and swirled down the streets of the towns, filling the air with dust so fine that it permeated buildings, clothing, granaries, and water tanks. Temperatures were as consistent as the wind—100° to 110°—and the humidity was so low that earth, boards, and even skin withered.

By the fall of 1918, it was clear that crisis was near at hand. The honyocker had no money for seed. A Shelby homesteader, working in Harlowton for enough money to plant in the spring of 1919, received a letter from his wife: "Today I have found the mares dead on the range, and the colt in the same condition . . . the cattle are dying. What is to be done?" Even with seed money, he now had no way to plant.

Governor Samuel Stewart's mail began to thicken with pleas from stricken farmers: "I have a mortgage of $1000

BEFORE "COUNTY SPLITTING," 1910
From a map prepared by Ellis Waldron

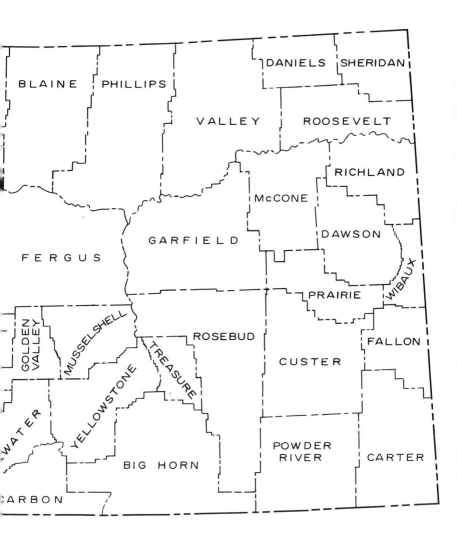

AFTER "COUNTY SPLITTING," 1922
From a map prepared by Ellis Waldron

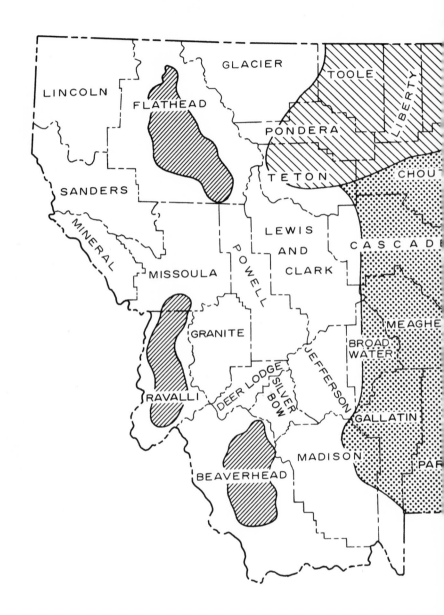

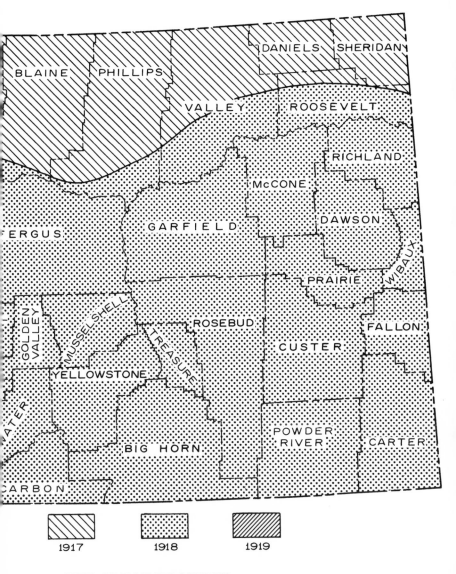

THE GREAT DROUGHT
From a map prepared by Ellis Waldron

against my land. The Peters Investment Company in Elmore, Minnesota, holds it. I need to borrow money for next year's seed, but I cannot even pay the interest due on the mortgage, and due to the last three crop failures, I owe $1300." From Dutton a bitter honyocker wrote, "A lot of settlers here have already moved to Canada for they say that the Canadian government is helping farmers much more than the United States government. Unless the government is willing to do something for the homesteaders here right soon, we will all have to nail up our windows and go."

The seed problem was acute. In Forsyth and Circle, farmers were $100,000 short of seed necessary to plant acreage which had been under cultivation; the Jordan Chamber of Commerce notified the governor that the "drought last year caused about 90 per cent failure, the $10,000 worth of county warrants for furnishing seed will cover only one-twentieth of the need." Professor F. S. Cooley of the State Extension Service, estimated that two million bushels of seed would be needed for the spring sowing in eastern Montana. *Farm, Stock and Home*, a Midwestern agricultural paper, estimated that a threatened loss in wheat production in eastern Montana because of the seed shortage would amount to 5,000,000 to 8,000,000 bushels—enough to feed the American Army in Europe for two years.

The honyocker *was* receiving both federal and state aid for seed. Between 1918 and 1920 he received $2,005,505 in seed loans—but the problem was not seed—it was the drought.

Chambers of commerce and promotional groups were loath to admit the fact. In Billings the chamber reported to the governor in 1919: "Individuals and companies heretofore contemplating starting new industries are being discouraged by grossly exaggerated reports of failure and ruin in this state." The governor should do something, the chamber reported, or Montana's reputation as a "stable farming and livestock area would be ruined in a few months."

The *Minneapolis Daily News* pooh-poohed the drought and said, "Don't pity Montana. . . . The wealth is there in a soil so rich and productive that you could just about take a sack of it to a bank in Belgium and draw interest on it." All Montanans had to do was stop complaining and "hang on, keep a stiff upper lip."

The governor's mail was now about evenly divided between anguished cries for help and outraged letters from various chambers and commercial clubs denying that a problem existed at all. By the spring of 1919, the latter type of communication had ceased entirely. The mail bags were full of demands for a special legislative session, for immediate action of some sort, for state loans.

Both U.S. Senators T. J. Walsh and H. L. Myers were involved. To a query from Walsh, the frustrated governor replied in June of 1919, "We have been expecting rain every day. It looks promising but nothing comes. I sincerely hope we may get some moisture before the . . . crop is entirely destroyed."

Senator Myers wired the governor on the third of July: "Am in receipt daily of letters and telegrams from Montana saying thousands of farmers and homesteaders with work teams and other livestock are facing starvation, and appealing for help. . . . What do state authorities intend to do? What would you suggest that I do?" To which the governor replied, "Do not know what you can do unless can secure reduced railroad rates for feed and livestock. Will write later as conditions develop."

"Conditions developed" with more winds, another invasion of grasshoppers, great "grass fires," in which the earth itself burned when the chalky grass had gone—and no rain—only the bright, glazed sky and the white-hot disc of the sun wheeling slowly over the earth.

With 3,000 foodless, seedless, landless, and money-less honyockers in Hill County alone, with letters and petitions and reports pouring into his office, Governor Stewart called a special session of the legislature in July, 1919. They convened and after much debate passed a law providing the county commissioners with the authority to issue bonds for additional road construction on the theory that destitute honyockers could be hired for road work. No one wanted the bonds, and little new construction was started. The legislative assembly, confronted with genuine crisis, solemnly debated the weather and adjourned.

Appeals to the Red Cross proved fruitless. After examining the stricken area, the Red Cross informed the governor that "The drought was not a sudden catastrophe which left the community disorganized and incapable of pulling itself together." Officials of the Red Cross also stated that the care of "drought sufferers was primarily a state concern, the state being interested in maintaining the vigor of its rural settlers purely as a matter of investment."

The exodus had started late in the fall of 1917; by the summer of 1918 it was well underway; by the summer of 1919 it was a flood. They left not as they had come but on the rods, or bundled in empty freight cars. A few of them still had worn-out trucks or cars which they piled high with their own and their neighbors' goods and, leaving a cloud of dust behind them, lopsidedly and slowly they headed west or north—or anywhere. The continuing drought and the ceaseless wind battered their deserted houses, shrank their deserted towns, and blew the soil they had so arduously plowed eastward in great gray clouds across the horizon. The dark wind denuded 2,000,000 acres and partially destroyed millions more.

III

The banker in Gilman, Montana, bought a book in 1912 entitled *How to Increase a Bank's Deposits*. In 128 pages, it delineated eighteen ways to advertise. The Gilman bank opened in 1910 and failed in 1923. In spite of the do-it-yourself approach aimed at increasing deposits, the Gilman bank, like hundreds of other new banking enterprises, was better at loaning money than at attracting depositors.

Between 1920 and 1926, more than half of Montana's commercial banks failed. In this six-year period, 214 banks closed their doors, never to reopen. Of these banks, 191 had failed by the closing months of 1924, more than a third of all the banks in the state.

The Superintendent of Banks in Montana described the period from 1920 to 1924 as "one long dripping tunnel—a veritable nightmare." Of the 277 state (as distinct from national) banks reporting to his office in 1921, as required by law, 85 had less than the required legal reserves; 181 had not been examined by the banking department at all, and those that were examined were found to be full of "second mortgages, frozen assets, land contracts, commission notes and whatnot."

Overleaf: Homesteaders Edgar Stauffer, "Happy Jack," and John Dobler, "Spider," in Stillwater County. *Courtesy Montana Historical Society.*

ks Bush Day

Montana was not alone in its trauma. In 1920 there was a worldwide decline in agricultural prices. An economically resurgent Europe concentrated on increased agricultural production, and by 1925 that production had reached its pre-war level. There was a steadily decreasing need for American farm products.

Nonetheless, immediately following the end of the war, the

First National Bank, Hardin. *Courtesy Montana Historical Society.*

United States engaged in (and banks participated in) what the Federal Reserve Board called "an unprecedented orgy of extravagance, a mania for speculation, [which] overextended business in nearly all lines and in every section of the country." A Congressional investigating committee in 1921 described the activity as characterized by "expansion, extravagance, and speculation, the like of which has never been seen in this country or the world."

Banks everywhere had loaned money on war-inflated commodity and land values—and banks everywhere failed as a consequence. But not as they failed in Montana and not with the same effect.

Montana was heavily "over-banked." State banking regulations were similar to federal regulations, although supervision was strikingly lax. In 1917 the Comptroller of the Currency chartered 176 new banks in the United States. Forty-one were in Montana, which already had more than a full quota of state banks. The town of Belt (population 1,000) had two state banks in 1917 when the Comptroller of the Currency issued a charter for a new national bank. Stanford (population 300) had a bank that had been operating since 1911, yet a national bank was chartered in 1916. Great Falls (population 20,000) had three state and two national banks; a third national bank was established in 1917.

National banks were all members of the Federal Reserve System, and it is difficult to avoid the conclusion that Montana's "over-banked" condition of 1920 was due to federal as much as to state foolishness in granting bank charters. National banks were at a competitive disadvantage with state banks until the Federal Reserve Act of 1913, but thereafter they entered the field with an aggressiveness unbecoming their self-asserted conservatism.

Yet the banks that failed in Montana had several distinct characteristics in common: more state banks failed than national; more small banks failed than large; more country banks failed than city banks; more new banks failed than old; more failed east of the Continental Divide than west.

There is little doubt but that most of the failed banks also shared in common mismanagement, or at least inexperienced management. Loans had been made on insufficient collateral, and reserves were not adequate.

Yet behind these facts stands another. Small banks in eastern and central Montana lacked the ability to diversify their earning assets. They were singularly dependent on the local economy. Behind *that* fact stands the spectre of drought and an undiversified agricultural economy, both of which were abetted by grossly inflated commodity and land values.

Once it had started, it spread like the drought. Those whom the banker owed called for payment; he called in his notes—he foreclosed. The depositors' nerves tightened and they began withdrawing. Eastern depositors, particularly, forced him to divert earning assets quickly into cash to provide for withdrawals. Moreover, many banks had sold farm mortgages to investors with a guarantee that they would pay the principal and interest. Now, as payments were suspended, the banker had to convert further earning assets into cash.

The loss of confidence was contagious. Before the wave had crested and bank doors started closing, even before the average Montanan knew that there was trouble, there had been an eastward flow of $30,000,000 in Montana bank deposits. The bankers fell back on the only reserve they had left—Liberty Bonds. It was not enough; foreclosure, forced sale, foreclosure and forced sale.

In the end Montana lost some 11,000 farms; farm mortgage indebtedness reached $175,000,000; the bankruptcy rate was the highest in the United States; the great bulk of the total bankruptcies in the state's history date to this period. The average value of farm land in the state was cut in half; farm tenantry increased fivefold between 1910 and 1925; one quarter of all foreclosures were by non-Montanans.

In the long aftermath, Montanans continued to argue about the disaster. There was ironic comfort in the fact that the whole nation suffered a similar ordeal in the early thirties. By then, Montanans knew all there was to know about the agony of bank failures.

They tended, as is almost always the case with people who are passing through a bewildering nightmare, to oversimplify. Increasingly, in the late twenties and early thirties, they pointed an accusing finger at the Federal Reserve Board. But it was left to an angry and controversial writer, Joseph Kinsey Howard, to sum up the bitter resentment of many Montanans.

In *Montana: High, Wide, and Handsome*, published in 1943, Howard lashed out at the policies of the Federal Reserve Board, which, he said, "set out coldly and deliberately to smash prices, including the inflated agricultural values its wartime credit policy had helped to establish; and despite its protestations to the contrary, it did this with brutal haste."[1] He accused the system of "relentlessly squeezing agricultural paper out of the rural banks of the northwest," leaving them without "adequate economic function in their communities." He charged the system with being wholly oriented toward Eastern business and manufacturing interests with callous indifference toward agriculture and the West. Not only, said Howard, did they damage the rural banks with a sharp rise in the rediscount rates, they turned the screws even further by demanding "additional collateral," which "appeared to Montanans then [1920], and appears still, to be nothing more nor less than a racket, a gigantic shakedown, which helped to break more than a third of Montana's banks . . . and which was the second phase of the economic destruction of a

[1] See Joseph Kinsey Howard, *Montana: High, Wide, and Handsome* (New Haven, Yale University Press, 1943), Chapters XX and XXI.

The first state bank in Montana, at Big Sandy. *Courtesy Montana Historical Society.*

state. . . ." This additional collateral scheme, said Howard, was devised to pull the last assets from the rural banks, Liberty Bonds, which the "system" then discounted 80 cents on the dollar.

Howard's book had a wide sale in Montana. His attack on the Federal Reserve's role in the Montana disaster was detailed, bitter, and vividly written, and to many Montanans his explanation of the role of the Federal Reserve stands today as an accurate and complete representation of the catastrophe. For many it answered all the questions and confirmed the belief that the ordeal was, after all, traceable to exploitative "outside" interests. The drought and drastically falling wheat prices faded into the background in the minds of many Montanans. So did their own wild speculation. It was easier to deal with a conspiracy by men than the cycles of nature and complex world economic conditions.

It is true that the new Federal Reserve Board was inexperienced. It is true, too, that it may not have functioned as it might have to relieve the crushing deflation of the early twenties. Yet it is doubtful that Howard's description of the role played by the Federal Reserve is accurate. Easy credit to banks that were grossly overextended would doubtless have saved very few of them. Moreover, it will not do to read today into yesterday. Humane social policies, in government and business, were simply not part of the picture in the 1920's. The average American's respect for the marketplace was immense and controlling.

In his bitterness, Joseph Kinsey Howard overlooked several fundamental facts. In early 1920 wheat was selling on the Minneapolis Grain Exchange at $3.30 per bushel. By late 1920 it had dropped to $1.46, and by early 1921, to $1.40. The Federal Reserve Board could do nothing at all about the fact that faith in the price of wheat and faith in the Montana banks were, in essence, the same thing. And it was resurgent European agricultural production, not Federal Reserve policies, that led to plummeting wheat prices.

Nor did Howard investigate the actual role of the Federal Reserve Bank of Minneapolis and the Ninth Federal Reserve District. From 1921 through 1929, 20 of every 100 banks in America failed. In the Ninth District, the rate was the highest in the nation: 31 per cent failed in Minnesota, 62 per cent in North Dakota, and 70 per cent in South Dakota and Montana. Yet the Federal Reserve Bank of Minneapolis, by mid-1920, had loaned to weakened member banks so much money that its gold reserves stood at the legal minimum. By August, 1921, it had loaned $13,601,252 to Montana banks. This was three times the amount of the reserves of the Montana member banks as of that date. In other words, it is difficult to see what more the Minneapolis bank could have done.

Howard did not accurately describe the actual condition of the Montana banks before the main wave of failures began. On June 20, 1921, there were 420 banks in Montana. The total deposits for all of these banks were just $2,000,000 more than the total loans, *creating an over-all ratio of loans to deposits of 98.6 per cent.* Then, now, or one hundred years ago, that is a ratio that would make the hair of even the most inveterate banking speculator stand on end. Worse, in nearly 50 per cent of the banks, loans exceeded deposits, often by very wide margins. For instance, in December, 1922, the Stockmen's National Bank of Fort Benton, Montana, had deposits amounting to $702,000 and loans amounting to $1,427,000. The bank failed in 1924.

The Federal Reserve Board's wartime loose-credit policies

can in no sense explain away or justify the condition of most Montana banks in the early 1920's because there is simply no evidence that the board countenanced the wild speculation of which the Montana banks were a symptom.

IV

The bank failures and the exodus of the honyockers, however, told only part of the story. They presaged greater and more lasting losses. Between 1914 and 1922, the state's population increased but 23 per cent, while the cost of county administration rose by 149 per cent; highways, bridges, and ferries, 138 per cent; education, schools, and libraries, 172 per cent; and "miscellaneous expenses" by 587 per cent.

This was the consequence of "county-splitting." Between 1910 and 1925 the honyockers carved twenty-eight new counties out of the old ones in Montana. It was understandable that everyone wanted to be closer to a county seat; it was understandable that new counties reflected high optimism. But county-splitting soon became a promoter's dream. For a fee, the promoter would begin the action. He would produce better roads, bridges, and services of all kinds. County-splitting meant new jobs, new towns, profit, and "progress." County-splitting meant growth and growth meant county-splitting. And so the promoters formed groups, collected fees, and beseiged the legislatures.

Until 1915, the legislature kept tight control over the creation of new counties. Indeed, one can hardly visualize a more fundamental obligation of government than rigidly to control the method and criteria for subdividing itself. Yet the legislature in 1915 divested itself of this obligation and with the passage of the Leighton Act abdicated its responsibility to the existent counties themselves. Thus, like the amoeba, counties began to multiply, aided by the machinations of the county-splitters. All that was necessary for a county to divide was for certain minimum property evaluations to exist in the proposed new (and old) county areas and for petitions to be signed and elections to be held. This was grist for the promoter's mill.

So, the counties were created, new courthouses were built, new sheriffs and clerks were hired, filing cabinets were ordered, new roads, bridges, and schools came into existence, new surveys were made by new surveyors, new judges ordered new benches—and new taxes, many new taxes, were levied to pay for it all.

It was "progress"; it was "growth," and then the honyockers left. But the new counties stayed, and the cost of maintaining them stayed also. It has been with Montanans ever since. Because the increased taxation fell almost exclusively upon property (there was no other source) the real effect of the legislature's default in 1915 was that government began confiscating private property via tax sales to maintain the cost of government itself. Taxes per acre quickly rose 140 per cent. Delinquency in eastern and central Montana became the common order of the day—so much so that in many areas the county became practically the only landholder. Over-all, county land ownership increased nearly 5,000 per cent with a concomitant drop in the valuation of farm land of $320,000,000 and a delinquency account of $18,000,000. No one has yet calculated the long-term cost of county-splitting, but in its sad history of head-in-the-sand politics, apathy, and paralysis, the Leighton Act stands out in the annals of legislative history as a landmark.

Overleaf: Farm machinery for sale in eastern Montana, about 1925. *Courtesy University of Montana Library.*

93

The story of the honyocker is thus one of ramified complexity. His failure, which was rooted in an ignorance of the land, its limitations and its history, involved not just the land and himself but, ultimately, the entire economy of the state. No Montanan escaped the consequences, long and short range. Participating with him in gross miscalculation were businessmen, cattle ranchers, industry, and government. Perhaps it was inevitable that the narrow margins of Montana's economy and its dependence not only on quixotic nature but on economic strings pulled far from the local scene would rupture. Yet a promotional campaign was clearly translated into public policy and it is difficult to avoid the conviction that had this not been the case, the consequences would have been far less severe.

Agricultural scientists were not without blame. Too often they lent their names to the promotion. As scientists they had no long-run, experimental evidence, no comparative statistics, no solid studies of other regions upon which to base any endorsement of mass settlement on the semiarid plains. Too often they gave that endorsement.

Out of the tragedy there slowly and painfully arose a new approach based on adaptation, drought- and rust-resistant wheat, strip farming of very large acreages, highly mechanized operations, and scientifically sound tillage and moisture-conserving practices. The weapons in the arsenal of today's wheat farmer are impressive. When the wet cycle returned in the 1940's, the new wheat farmer set impressive records. From 1938 to 1949 the annual average production of wheat was 67,000,000 bushels. In 1950 the old honyocker area produced an all-time record of 93,950,000 bushels.

Yet it would behoove the wheat farmer of today occasionally to stop by the ruins of his predecessor. His success is built on those ruins—and there is great danger in short memories. One of the students of the period wrote in 1957: "Yet once more the pressure to pyramid quick profits has brought a tendency to dismiss the protective features. Large areas of pasture land have been put into cultivation; strip farming is too frequently limited to the confines of the soil conservation districts; fallow fields are too often left in weeds throughout the summer. Farmers have expanded operations beyond their capacity for sound workmanship and beyond the margins of long-term yield expectancy."[2]

The Montana wheat farmer of today can ill afford to forget the honyocker. Whatever agricultural science and government have done for him, the drought will come again, a fierce and implacable visitation; there is no real substitute for rain; there is no real way to stop the wind or cool the sun. The blowing of soil is not a momentary phenomenon; it is a chronic disease that afflicts cultivated areas in semiarid regions—and remission is not a cure. Let today's Montanan stop occasionally by the remnants of the honyocker's town, with its blankly staring windows, its collapsed granary, occupied only by field mice and prairie dogs, and its bank—the door agape, the vault empty. It is important to remember.

Only this need be added: According to the 1970 census, Montana's per capita income has fallen from thirteenth to forty-third and its population growth has been far below the national average. The new state Department of Economic Planning, the governor, and various other groups are now cooking up all manner of plans to attract people and industry to Montana (in the face of very considerable conservation

---

[2] Mary Wilma Hargreaves, *Dry Farming in the Northern Great Plains* (Cambridge, Harvard University Press, 1957), p. 22.

opposition). Whatever they do and however they do it, old-time Montanans in abundance still remember the great "boom" of the twenties and ardently hope that the planners and the politicians will not press the resources of the state beyond their capacity to sustain growth. And that capacity is limited.

IV. THE GREAT SHUTDOWN

> These people are my enemies—fierce, bitter, implacable. But they are your enemies, too. If they crush me today, they will crush you tomorrow. . . . They will force you to dwell in Standard Oil houses while you live—and they will bury you in Standard Oil coffins when you die.
>
> F. Augustus Heinze, Speech from the steps of the Butte Courthouse, October, 1903

THE plainsman—honyocker, rancher, banker, merchant, and speculator—had had his travail in the twenties. Although he had momentarily sought relief from the legislature and had used that body's apathy to pry new counties from old, he seldom looked westward. He was, indeed, almost wholly unaware of the pot that periodically boiled over in Helena and elsewhere in western Montana. This was not primarily due to distance, but rather to the fact that he had always looked eastward. It was the Congress that determined how the public domain was to be handled, not the state government. It was Congress, not the legislature, whom he petitioned; it was the railroads, Eastern owned and Eastern managed, not the Anaconda Copper Mining Company that had fingers in his pie. His affinity with kindred souls in western North and South Dakota was strong. They had bitter experiences in common and they had shared the same hopes and seen the same promises wither away.

Not so with the westerner, sealed off in his valleys, preoccupied with immense mining and lumbering enterprises, essentially inured from drought, one high and formidable mountain range removed from the outer rim of the desert.

The mountain Montanan was a different breed—and perhaps the greatest difference was that he could not look off across his countryside and, except for the bending of the earth, see all the way to Minneapolis. His eye was stopped short by the mountains and the forests. Unlike the plains Montanan, he did not squint; he was not wind- and sun-beaten. He looked more inward than outward. It was not that he was more parochial, nor was it wholly a matter of geography. The seat of power for the plainsman lay outside his region, and it was thus that he looked outward. The seat of power for the mountain Montanan was close and local—and so he looked inward.

The roots of settlement in Montana sank much deeper in time in the western valleys than on the plains. While buffalo still grazed by the thousands in the east, there were cities in

Transporting power-plant boilers in January, 1916. The trip took eighty-four days. *Courtesy Montana Historical Society.*

the mountain west—crude, perhaps, but roaring and teeming, nonetheless. By 1884 the world's largest copper smelter at Anaconda was belching smoke and spewing arsenic across the Deer Lodge valley. By 1888 the Copper Kings, Marcus Daly and William Andrews Clark, were locked in bitter combat and politics on every level revolved around them. By 1894 Helena had more millionaires, per capita, than any other city in America. And from 1880 to 1900 the wondrously productive and ingeniously managed Anaconda Copper Mining Company, a local corporation partly owned and entirely operated by Montanans, extended itself into every facet

Overleaf: Interior of the engine house in the Bimetallic Mine, Granite, about 1900. *Courtesy University of Montana Library.*

BiMETALLic Mine

of the lives of the western inhabitants. It was the most productive copper enterprise in the world. It owned millions of acres of timber; it owned municipal water works, stores, hotels, newspapers—ultimately all but one of the seven major dailies. It owned street railway systems, railroads, great sawmills, brickyards, and scores of other enterprises. By 1900 Anaconda was employing nearly three-quarters of the wage earners of the state.

From 1888 to 1900, the "Company," in the figure of Marcus Daly, involved itself in every aspect of politics, from the wards to the governorship and the election of U.S. senators. Daly threw its resources profligately into his political battle with W. A. Clark. The result, for most Montanans, was high entertainment, for a few, vast wealth, but it resulted in massive corruption of the machinery of government.

Montanans enjoyed the battle of the titans and even in the perspective of time look upon this dramatic period with fond indulgence. More has been written about the "War of the Copper Kings" than about any other period in the state's history, except perhaps the Indian wars and the Custer massacre. There is some justification for this, because whatever else it was, it was a home-grown war which rose out of home-grown business enterprises and was fought by Montanans. Whatever the Anaconda Copper Mining Company became, until 1900 it was a rare Montanan who did not look upon it, and its remarkable development, with a possessive pride.

But when the Standard Oil Company purchased the Anaconda Company in 1899, it formed a holding company, the Amalgamated Copper Company. Under the umbrella of this vast device it reached out for other companies and allied enterprises in Montana. In due course it absorbed the extensive holdings of William Andrews Clark. More significantly, however, it purchased the Boston and Montana Company, a large property in Butte financed exclusively by Boston bankers. Amalgamated's intentions (or rather, Standard Oil's) were no secret. H. H. Rogers, the great trust's president, had in mind a copper trust, intimately tied to the already enormous oil trust. The addition of the Boston and Montana was simply another step in Rogers' carefully laid plans.

Standard Oil had done its homework. Although within a year of Amalgamated's formation, vast stock-watering schemes disrupted the world's copper market, there is no doubt that Rogers knew within a few dollars the exact worth of his burgeoning copper empire. Nor is there any doubt that he was aware that the political warfare between Daly and Clark would in some measure extend itself into Amalgamated's affairs. Indeed, Daly himself, ill though he was in April, 1899, when Amalgamated was formed, remained as president of the operating company, Anaconda.

Amalgamated's officers (H. H. Rogers, William G. Rockefeller, Albert C. Burrage, and the president of New York's National City Bank, James Stillman) were among the most prestigious financiers in America. It is doubtful that they regarded the reports of conflict in Montana extending back into the 1880's with any trepidation. They had early consulted with W. A. Clark; they found no factors in Clark's and Daly's feud which would disrupt Amalgamated. They knew of the somewhat bizarre activities of a young man allied with Clark, one F. Augustus Heinze, but they did not consider him a problem. They were wrong.

Overleaf: Mule-drawn ore cars on the 1,100-foot level of the Rarus mine in Butte. *Courtesy University of Montana Library.*

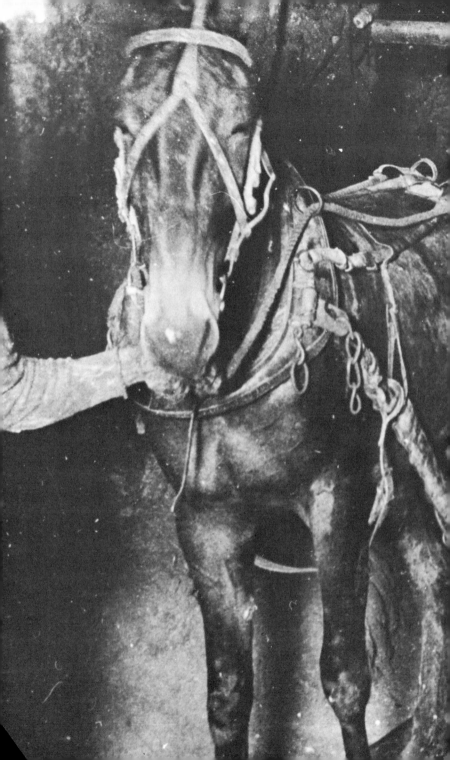

It was in their purchase of the Boston and Montana that they first encountered Heinze. The encounter was not at a conference table, but took place underground. Heinze busied himself with stealing Boston and Montana ore, tunneling in from his own property, the Rarus. The Boston and Montana people had previously sought to enjoin Heinze, but, as A. S. Bigelow, the former president of the Boston and Montana, explained to H. H. Rogers, the courts in Silver Bow County (Butte) were "somewhat peculiar."

In a short time, Rogers received information that Heinze was also tunneling into the enormously rich Piccolo and Gambetta veins (belonging to Amalgamated). Heinze had a cloudy title to a nearby claim, the Minnie Healy, and he simply veered off into the Amalgamated veins and, running twenty-four-hour shifts, purloined Amalgamated's copper with alarming efficiency and with startling rapidity.

Standard Oil had not become Standard Oil without a finely honed system for dealing with "industrial desperadoes." Indeed, the trust had a justifiable reputation for implacable ruthlessness. Even in an age when *laissez faire* was the economic order of the day, and financial and industrial enterprises were subject to no regulations and were restrained only by the limitations of fang and claw, Standard Oil was commonly credited with having "written the book." Its power and wealth were seemingly limitless. It must, therefore, have genuinely surprised Rogers and his officers when their initial moves to eliminate Heinze failed.

Marcus Daly died in November, 1900. Rogers could not turn to him, therefore, for advice on handling Heinze. He knew, however, that Heinze was largely financed by W. A. Clark. With Daly dead, Clark had no reason to support Heinze, who, in any event, had only served Clark as one weapon in the arsenal he reserved for Daly. It was not difficult for Rogers to split Clark from Heinze. Indeed, Clark was not only flattered by Rogers' attentions, he had already developed his plans to sell out to Amalgamated.

But Heinze was making money from his pirated ore. Nor was he without credit from the enemies of Standard Oil among Eastern financiers. The withdrawal of Clark's support had no visible effect on his activities.

By this time it had dawned on Amalgamated that the courts of Silver Bow County (Butte) were, indeed, as A. S. Bigelow had put it, "somewhat peculiar." There were two district court judges, William Clancy and Edward Harney. Both had been bought and paid for by F. Augustus Heinze. Moreover, Montana law made no provision for a change of venue if either party to a civil suit found the court prejudiced. Accordingly, all mining litigation in Silver Bow County came before Judge Clancy or Judge Harney—and no suit could be transferred elsewhere.

If Rogers and company had never heard of the "fearfully and wonderfully made" Apex Law prior to 1900, they must have had nightmares about it for the succeeding three years. The Apex Law, a clause in federal mining statutes, held, essentially, that if a vein of ore "apexed" or broke surface on a given claim, the owner of that claim had the right to follow that vein any distance underground as long as he remained within the fifteen-hundred-foot *length* of the surface claim. The law placed no restriction at all on the *lateral* variation of the vein.

Underground the Butte vein system was an incredible labyrinth of faulted and jumbled veins and ore bodies. The Apex Law, which made sense in mining districts where faulting had not scrambled the veins, was a farce in Butte, but it

109

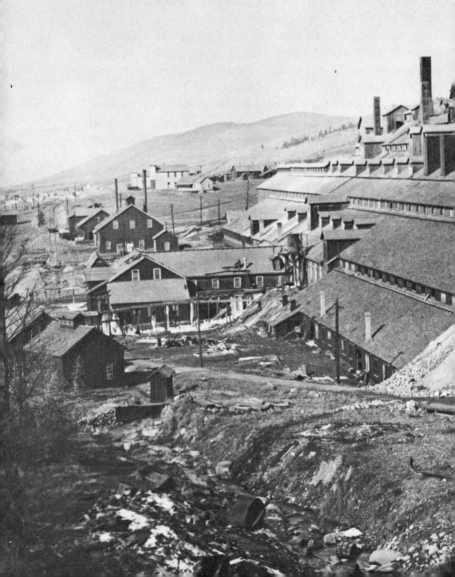

Bimetallic mill in Philipsburg, 1893.
Courtesy University of Montana Library.

lent some semblance of legal justification for the ponderings and ultimate decisions rendered by Judges Clancy and Harney.

While these decisions could be, and were, appealed to the Supreme Court, the process was ponderous—and Heinze continued meanwhile to steal hundreds of tons of rich ore. It was, in any event, Heinze's tactic to delay—a process in which Clancy and Harney were fully co-operative, Clancy often snoring loudly through hours of testimony, his head sunk on his uncombed beard.

By 1902, Heinze was involved in fourteen cases before the Supreme Court alone. He had thirty-seven attorneys on his staff who, all told, were involved in nearly one hundred law suits covering mining property that was valued at nearly $200,000,000.

Amalgamated, in an extraordinary move, took its case "to the people"—which must have raised a good many eyebrows in cynical surprise in New York financial circles. The trust had purchased Marcus Daly's *Anaconda Standard* with Anaconda's other properties. It was a good newspaper with impressive circulation in Butte, Anaconda, and Helena. Now Rogers began buying other papers—a network of dailies that covered the state leaving, ultimately, but one independent daily, *The Great Falls Tribune*.

But Heinze had his own newspaper, the *Reveille*. Characterized by invective without parallel in an age when invective was standard newspaper fare, the *Reveille*'s principal circulation was in Butte. But that, after all, was where it mattered. Amalgamated could revile Heinze all over the state; it could, and did, castigate Clancy and Harney; it could, and did, explain the essential absurdity of the legal grounds on which Heinze stood. It did not matter to Heinze, Clancy, or Harney and, perhaps more significantly, it did not matter to the miners and smeltermen of Butte and Anaconda. Heinze's charisma was extraordinary, and now, as an underdog fighting single-handedly the world's largest trust, the miners flocked to his standard wherever he planted it. He stopped the trust. Worse, the fight had attracted national attention. Not only was it front-page news in the big mining journals, it percolated into the New York newspapers and the popular magazines of the day. The widely read *Leslie's,* for example, commented "For he [Heinze] has made a more effective resistance to the deadening influence of Standard Oil domination than any other kind of man could possibly have done." *Leslie's* went on to describe Heinze as "both predatory and parasitic," but continued: "It is a fact that had he been a more scrupulous man, he would long since have been wiped off the slate. . . ."

Standard Oil was not unduly concerned about its "image," but Rogers was perfectly aware that the trust's critics on the national scene were not all without power, and always there loomed the threat of hostile federal legislation.

When Amalgamated failed to buy Judge Harney away from Heinze with the very considerable counter-offer of $250,000 for a favorable vote in the Minnie Healy case, all recourse save one had been resorted to. Amalgamated then took the step toward which it had been inexorably moving.

On October 22, 1903, the trust announced the total shutdown of all its enterprises in Montana except for its newspapers. Within a week some twenty thousand wage earners were out of work and near catatonic paralysis had beset Montana. The trust's newspapers carried exhaustive reviews of the machinations of F. Augustus Heinze which had led to the present state of affairs. William Scallon, Anaconda's president, went from his home to his office accompanied by a burly bodyguard.

F. Augustus Heinze took to the stump. He addressed a crowd of nearly ten thousand miners from the steps of the Butte courthouse, for example, and shouted: "If you wish to join hands with Amalgamated . . . and the Rockefellers and Rogers in driving me from the state of Montana, very well. It is your business. If you do, you will rue the day. . . ." The miners listened and when he had finished a great roar of support went up—but it was early in the game.

Democratic Governor Joseph K. Toole, whose relationship with Amalgamated had always been cool, found himself on the horns of a vicious dilemma. Letters and petitions poured into his office—and the early sentiment as expressed in this tonnage of mail was overwhelmingly against Amalgamated. The letters came from all over the state and from people in all walks of life; but there was little that he could do. Late in October he joined James J. Hill, president of the Great Northern Railroad, W. A. Clark, and Paris Gibson, on a mediation committee which sought to bring Heinze and William Scallon of Anaconda to the bargaining table. The attempt failed.

On October 31, the committee announced: "We have failed to obtain a stipulation from the parties litigant which will insure a resumption of work by the Amalgamated Copper Company, and have been unable to devise any plan looking to that end. . . ." On that same day, Amalgamated announced its own plan. William Scallon, in a personal statement which ran in a black-lined box on the front page of the *Standard*, set forth Amalgamated's terms: If the governor would promptly call a special session of the legislature and if that session would pass a "fair trials bill" stipulating that there could be a change of venue if either party to a civil suit considered the judge corrupt or prejudiced, Amalgamated would resume operations. Montana could go back to work.

Now Amalgamated's press began a concerted campaign to force the governor's hand. But it did not stop there. The trust's agents appeared all over the state with handily prepared petitions. On identically printed forms, these documents with thousands of signatures poured into the governor's office from the Belt, Montana farmers, the businessmen of Montana, the citizens of Shelby, Cut Bank, Browning, and Blackfoot, the residents of Silver Bow County, taxpayers of Powell County, and from labor organizations as well as businessmen. The volume of the governor's mail, which was already great, increased sharply. Though there were still violent protests and even some petitions encouraging the governor to resist Amalgamated's demands, throughout the dwindling days of the fall the pressure on Joseph K. Toole continued to grow and intensify.

The independent press, with the significant exception of *The Great Falls Tribune*, left no doubt as to the sentiments of country and small-town editors. Even in the eastern part of the state, the reaction was sharp and bitter. The *Lewistown Democrat* said: "The Amalgamated Company deserves the most unsparing censure for throwing thousands of men out of work for the sole purpose of securing political advantage." *The Flathead Herald Journal* remarked: "We believe that a deep, dark, damnable game is being played." The *Columbian* of Columbia Falls remarked, "The poor, persecuted people who control the Amalgamated Copper Company have discovered many defects in our judicial system which they desire the people to remedy at once . . . a word to the wise ought to be sufficient. Do we dare to risk the consequences of further offending these gentlemen?" The far-off *Spokesman Review* called Amalgamated's action "little short of criminal," and added "The people of the Northwest are likely to regard trusts and large aggregations of capital with greater disfavor than ever."

Once again the national press turned its attention to Montana. A release from the Boston News Bureau said, "The only question remaining is: Can Amalgamated with its inherited Standard Oil policy afford to admit the principle of arbitration? The people of Montana and possibly of the whole United States may ask: Can Amalgamated and its Standard Oil managers afford to reject it?" The *Boston Beacon* remarked: "The effect of this act is to bring home to the body of the people their dependence on the good will of the trust."

The shutdown had now been in effect for more than a month. It involved roughly four-fifths of the wage earners of the state. The paralysis extended itself into almost every business, large and small. Many miners and smeltermen, always a peripatetic breed, had left the state for Idaho or Arizona, and a bleak somnolence settled over Butte and Anaconda. Men were increasingly resentful and with empty larders and pockets began slowly to resent Heinze as well as Amalgamated. There were skeleton crews in the woods camps to the west and the unemployed loggers clustered in the streets of Missoula and other logging towns, or departed for Idaho. The governor's mail was heavy now with pleas for a quick special session. A letter from a Missoulian was typical: "I do hope you can see your way clear to call an extra session for I have to say that owing to the suspension by the Amalgamated people, I am out of employment, a condition that certainly worries a man with a wife and two children. My employment would not have been with Amalgamated people

116

either, but with others so affected by their closing as to be unable to keep their employees."

In Great Falls, a suspended effigy of Judge Clancy drew a sullen crowd to Central Avenue and Second Street, and the *Great Falls Leader* remarked that "The figure is well made up and depicts the Heinze Court even to his flowing whiskers and unpolished boots."

In Butte, William Scallon, who had replaced Marcus Daly as the president of Anaconda, looked out over an immobilized city from his office window on the sixth floor of the Hennesey Building. The gallows frames were stark against the November sky, now free from smoke and steam clouds, and he found the utter stillness disquieting. He did not like Heinze, and as an experienced mining lawyer, he had contempt for the corrupt courts. But neither did he like what he, Scallon, was doing. When the extra session was called (and he was sure it would be) and the special bill was passed, he intended to sever all connections with Anaconda and Amalgamated. He wanted to live in Butte for the rest of his life, and this was too much to stomach.

On November 10, Governor Toole yielded and set the convening of the special session for December 1. In the ensuing twenty days the pot boiled fiercely. F. Augustus Heinze scurried about the state setting up an antitrust party to convene in Helena at the same time as the special session. A quick count of the votes in the legislature revealed that that body was prepared to pass the fair trials bill overwhelmingly. Not, indeed, that there was no opposition, but the agitation was largely rhetorical.

Overleaf: The Little Ben mine, Little Rockies. *Courtesy Montana Historical Society.*

In both his proclamation convening the session and in his message addressed to it on December 1, the governor controlled his bitterness. He simply set forth the problem, and in his ten-minute message remarked: "The situation calls for the exercise of consummate skill and judgment on your part." He did not mention Amalgamated and made no recommendations of his own. He said, "I must assume that those who by petitions and otherwise have been insistent upon calling you together will find and formulate an adequate remedy; but whatever form it takes, *it must be remembered that you are legislating for the future of the whole state* [italics mine]."

Early in the session, William Whitely, a representative from Silver Bow County, introduced a resolution stating that "No extra session of the legislature [presumably in the future] should or ought to be called at any time at the threat, behest, or command of any corporation, person or persons." The resolution was promptly defeated by the house, twenty-four to twelve.

Meanwhile, Heinze's antitrust delegates arrived in Helena and went into formal session on December 7. There were 650 delegates from all over the state. The first order of business was to provide for a verbatim record of the proceedings, "it being impossible for the people of Montana to learn the facts in matters of public interest from the daily press owned and controlled by the Amalgamated Copper Company."

The Company press was joined by several independent papers, including *The Great Falls Tribune*, in claiming that the expenses of the delegates to the antitrust convention were paid by Heinze. Many of the delegates were undoubtedly subsidized by Heinze, but others stoutly and indignantly denied that such was the case. After several days of rousing and often violently recriminatory speeches, the convention produced a platform for the new Anti-Trust party. Though the platform centered on assertions that corporate influence in Montana politics was an unmitigated evil and that Amalgamated should be driven from the political scene, it also contained recommendations for the initiative and referendum, revision of the hodgepodge mine taxation laws, the creation of a railroad and public service regulatory commission, and an employer liability law. Thus, the first concrete proposals involving Montana in the progressivism then sweeping the United States arose from the antitrust convention. But the convention did not influence the legislature, nor did it result in a third party movement. Three days after its platform was printed, the legislature passed the fair-trials bill, and on December 10 adjourned. The representatives went home; Amalgamated gave the signal, and Montana went back to work.

Heinze lingered on for a few years, but all of his power was gone. He sold out to Amalgamated in 1906 for $10,000,-000 (his nuisance value, as his friends called it) and went to New York where he died in 1914.

Looking back on this period, Burton K. Wheeler remarked in his autobiography, *Yankee from the West*, ". . . the lesson for Butte was clear. No matter how clever, unscrupulous or spendthrift the opponent, you couldn't lick Amalgamated." But it was far more than a lesson for Butte. It was lesson for all of Montana, brutally and cynically exercised with swift ruthlessness. Montanans learned that lesson well, and nothing attests to that fact quite as adequately as the conduct of the state's legislature for years to come.

Bodies politic, as well as people, have memories. Legislative bodies, in particular, have traditions and characteristics deeply rooted in the past. The stamp of subservience which

121

dated to the special session of 1903 remained in livid outline for years to come. When, under intense federal pressure in 1915, Amalgamated dissolved itself and Standard Oil got out of Montana, the operating company, Anaconda, took over. But that made little difference to Montanans. Anaconda had a memory, too. The "Company" never let things get far out of hand. In all essential respects it controlled the legislature, the press, and most facets of the economy of the state except for agriculture. It did not relax. William Scallon did resign. Even as late as 1947 he referred to the shutdown of 1903 with regret and distaste.

State legislatures are notable for the turnover of personnel. It can hardly be argued that the shutdown was much in the minds of legislators, say, in the 1930's and 1940's. Yet in combination with the overt employment of power and coercion by the Company throughout the years, it remained very much a part of the Montana psyche.

V. GIBRALTAR LAID LOW

> So long as they are here—just so long as they
> are here, let labor remember that they will pit the
> one of us against the other—and that way we will
> never, never win.
>
> Rae Logan, Charlo. Personal Interview

I F the shutdown of 1903 shocked Montanans in all walks
of life, its effect on organized labor was profound. Unions
themselves had participated in the campaign to pressure
Governor Toole into calling a special session. The internecine
struggle that ensued within labor organizations thereafter was
bitter. Yet far more serious was the blow to tradition, to a
belief that organized labor in Montana's mining industry was
strong, and that Butte was a "Gibraltar of Unionism."

Butte, after all, had been the birthplace of the great Western Federation of Miners, of which the Butte Union became
the first local in 1893. It was a veritable hub of unionism.
Its strength, so union men thought, had radiated outward to
all of western Montana, encompassing smeltermen and men
in the woods camps. It had percolated into the ranks of all
labor—or so union men believed.

Unionism had won its first triumph in Montana as early
as 1878 when the Butte Workingmen's Union struck at the
Alice and Lexington mines in protest over a wage cut. Led
by a brass band, about four hundred men marched down the
gulch from Walkerville to Butte carrying placards announcing a strike. The camp's weekly newspaper, the *Miner*, remarked cautiously, "It must be the constant care of its [the

union's] members to guard it from the faintest approach of anything smacking of communism." Yet the *Miner* did not condemn the new union even when many of the workers on the hill walked out in sympathy. "It will receive our support," said the paper, "so long as it eschews violence or coercion."

Butte's first strike lasted more than a month and although the ultimate settlement was something of a compromise, the *Miner* remarked, "It is almost a certainty that no other attempt to reduce wages will be made at an early date after so determined and well organized a resistance."

The *Miner* was correct. The lesson had not been lost on Marcus Daly, part owner and manager of the Alice. Not only was Daly a pragmatist to whom production mattered above all else, he identified closely with the workingmen. He had been a "hot-water boy" in the steaming sumps of Nevada's Comstock and he never forgot it. As he clawed his way upward in the early 1880's developing the giant Anaconda, his relationships with a growing army of miners and smeltermen remained universally good. By 1885 the Butte Miner's Union, as it was now called, stood high in the register of western unionism.

In 1888, when the War of the Copper Kings erupted, and as Daly's feud with William Andrews Clark broke into open warfare, Daly came to regard his employees as troops. They were to be well fed, well clothed, well treated, well paid—and they were to respond with their undivided loyalty. They did so, voting as a massive bloc, working in the interests of Daly's political purposes on every level, as well as in his mines.

Clark, and later F. Augustus Heinze, responded with similar programs. The eight-hour day came to Montana miners not as the result of pressure exerted by militant labor, but as a ploy by Clark and Heinze to outwit Daly in the widening

124

bid for the votes and support of laboring men. In the competition to outdo each other among the Copper Kings, labor could not lose. Indeed, it rarely had to ask. Paternalism is much too mild a word to describe the salubrious climate in which labor and unionism basked.

In the years from 1888 to 1900, Butte had no contractual closed shop because it was not needed. Non-union men simply did not fit into the scheme of things. While unions throughout the rest of the country were fighting bitter and bloody battles for the right to exist, the right to bargain collectively, the right to strike, unionism in Butte flourished. This was the period in which the myth of strength was rooted.

When Standard Oil bought Anaconda and when Amalgamated came onto the Montana scene, labor turned wary. In the period from 1900 to the shutdown of 1903, appearances rather than reality governed Butte unionism. There were harbingers of trouble aplenty, but a quiet kind of paralysis afflicted labor in Montana.

While peace and amity reigned between capital and labor in this "golden era" of Montana's labor history, violent conflict swirled around the perimeters. Unionism in Butte was imperfectly insulated. The Butte Miner's Union *had* become the first local of the regional Western Federation of Miners in 1893. The Butte local, indeed, did more to sustain it financially than any other. The Federation was militant, responding to situations outside of Montana very unlike those inside. The W.F.M. directed the bloody strikes at Coeur d'Alene in 1893 and 1899, at Cripple Creek in 1894 and 1903–1904, at Leadville in 1896–97, Salt Lake in 1899, Telluride in 1901, and Idaho Springs in 1903. These strikes were among the most violent and bloody in the history of the American labor movement. The Butte Miner's Union, as the richest local of

125

the W.F.M., stood apart from these conflicts only because of the unique developments in Montana—and only as long as the Copper Kings fought. In 1899 Standard Oil bought the Anaconda; in 1900 Marcus Daly died; in 1903 F. Augustus Heinze was destroyed by Amalgamated. There were no more perimeters.

Amalgamated brought no paternalistic philosophy into its Montana enterprise. On the contrary, it brought Standard Oil's ruthlessness, impersonalism, and icy efficiency. Its policy toward labor was formulated in New York and was based on an inherent hostility to labor organizations, to strikes, to bargaining.

Amalgamated's officials were perfectly aware of the labor violence boiling around the edges of Montana—in Idaho, Utah, and Colorado. They had studied the W.F.M. carefully. They were aware, too, that nowhere had the W.F.M. won the day when confronted with unified company opposition— and company opposition in all the areas under W.F.M. pressure had been unified, implacable, and victorious.

As of 1900, Amalgamated began to infiltrate the Butte Miner's Union with its own men, with trained detectives and with others instructed to sow dissension. By the time of the shutdown of 1903, Amalgamated was satisfied that labor would protest feebly at best. Their appraisal was accurate.

The W.F.M. was not unaware of the Butte local's paralysis and of Amalgamated's infiltration. As early as 1902 the *Miner's Magazine*, reflecting the views of the W.F.M., commented on company-minded men in the local and remarked, "Such imps in the robes of unionism should be relegated to the perdition of labor's damnation."

Increasingly, the Butte local found itself out of step with the W.F.M. It moved slowly to the right, while the Federation moved to the left. By 1905 the leadership of the local was predominantly "conservative," that is, it sought to maintain the status quo. Amalgamated had demonstrated its power in that black October two years previously, and the leadership of the local wanted no repetition.

The W.F.M., however, kept at its campaign to knock the Butte local off dead center. The *Miner's Magazine* harped at the issue of company infiltration: "The membership . . . must keep awake and no longer permit themselves to be chloroformed by a few 'gentlemen' in the Union, who have such a pull with the Amalgamated Copper Company that they are able to secure leases that net them competent bank accounts. These leases are the rewards paid for shaping the policy of the Union."

A crisis occurred in 1906. Since the early 1890's the wage of the miner had been a flat $3.50 per day. The cost of living had risen steadily and by the fall of 1906 the union was ready to ask for an increase. They presented Amalgamated with a demand for 50 cents; John D. Ryan, Anaconda's president, countered with an offer of 25 cents. The "conservative" leadership of the union not only accepted Ryan's counter-offer, but at a meeting which appeared to the "dissidents" to be completely "stacked," tendered a vote of thanks to the Company. This nearly tore the union asunder because it confirmed in the minds of many members a growing conviction that the organization was really controlled by the Company, a view assiduously cultivated by the W.F.M.

Confronted by this schism, the leadership moved right, and a hard core of the membership moved left. The hard core held out for a strike and began to gather support.

At this juncture the Company employed a tactic it was to use again and again in its relationships with labor throughout

127

the years, a tactic which ultimately became monotonous in its predictability. In late November, 1906, it suspended all operations in the mines, explaining the action as a necessary consequence of "full ore bins." The memory of October, 1903, was too fresh; the move for a strike promptly collapsed. The conservative leadership within the union remained in firm control, and Amalgamated re-opened the mines.

What might have happened in Montana had the Industrial Workers of the World not entered the picture is problematical. There may, in any event, have been little chance for labor to have dealt rationally at any time with Amalgamated. But the I.W.W. did appear, and it appeared on a scene already fluid and greatly confused.

Founded in 1905 in Chicago, the Industrial Workers of the World represented discordant and disgruntled elements of the American labor movement. They were radical, alienated, and angry. They had in mind a nationwide industrial union. Their aim was Marxist, the creation of a working-class movement, anti-capitalist, anti-free enterprise, revolutionary.

At the original convention, Charles Moyer and William D. Haywood represented the Western Federation of Miners, the only organization officially represented, all other delegates attending as individuals. It was a prestigious gathering of radicals, including Eugene V. Debs, Ernest Unterman of the Socialist party, and many others. It was immediately clear that the goal of the organization was not merely to advance the cause of labor, but to destroy the capitalistic system and substitute for it an industrial organization of workers.

Even here, however, schism quickly developed and the I.W.W. split into left and right. The Western Federation of Miners bolted the organization. It was unwilling to go as far or as fast as the radicals proposed. The I.W.W.'s, or "Wob-

128

blies," as they came to be called, occupied the extreme left of the American labor movement, openly violent advocates of class warfare, utterly intransigent.

Between 1908 and 1916, this radical organization attracted public attention in the nation as a whole and particularly in the West, where they concentrated on lumberjacks, migratory fruit pickers, and miners.

From beginning to end, the number of Wobblies in Montana was grossly exaggerated. Yet by 1912 they were nonetheless beginning to wreak havoc. Their intent was to capture, or at least to disrupt, the W.F.M. locals, and Butte was a focal point of their attack.

In the Butte local, the "conservatives" still held a slippery command of the union in 1912. In the election of officers that year, a slate was chosen utterly unacceptable to the left. The defeated candidate of the left, Tom Campbell, appeared at the W.F.M. convention that year and demanded that President Moyer take the affairs of the local out of the hands of the present officers who had been placed in office "through and by the efforts of the mining companies of Butte." Campbell spoke to the convention, asking for an investigation of the Butte case by the W.F.M. He said, "If you do . . . investigate, I will venture to say that what part you will find of the men who are responsible for the making of that organization are today at the mercy of the corporations and their pets, which they would not be if the general organization [W.F.M.] showed any desire to render any assistance to the ambitious, class conscious, sincere workers against the insatiable greed of the Amalgamated Copper Company."

Overleaf: The gold dredge *Mosier* at Pioneer City, about 1900. *Courtesy University of Montana Library.*

But the W.F.M., Moyers in particular, believed Campbell to be an I.W.W. They had bolted that organization years before. They promptly expelled Campbell from the W.F.M. by a vote of 198 to 26—leaving the "conservatives" still at the helm of the Butte local.

Late in 1912 the Company instituted the "rustling-card" system. By virtue of this device, a miner had to procure a "rustling card" from the employment office before he could look for work on "the hill." If he got the job, the card was deposited with the mine foreman, who then returned it to the employment office. Detailed dossiers were kept on all employees, and the Company was thus able to control all personnel in the mines and to turn away "undesirables."

This struck at the heart of what strength the union had. The union itself was heavily infiltrated with Company men; remarks hostile to Company policy quickly led to a denial of a rustling card. A man either watched his tongue and held his job or spoke out and lost it. New union recruits quickly learned that to side with the left meant no card and no job.

What was now called "the Company slate" still controlled the union, its power residing in the desire of a majority of the members to work. More and more, suspicion controlled union activities. If a man worked on the hill, could he be other than a Company man? If he was in the union could he be other than a "stooge"? If he had no rustling card, did he carry the "red card" of the Wobblies?

On the afternoon of June 13, 1914, the annual Miner's Union Day parade, which had always been a festive occasion for all of Butte, began its march down the main street. Led by the carriage of Frank J. Hayes, vice-president of the United Mine Workers of America, who was to be the speaker of the day, the parade was more like the advance of a grim brigade.

The bystanders were silent and uneasy, the marchers were on the alert for trouble. Conspicuously absent from the ranks of the marchers were the "progressives."

As the parade approached the corner of Park and Dakota streets, a mob surged in from Park Street. The union leaders were de-horsed and chaos broke out in the streets. The sheriff, Tim Driscoll, was brushed aside, and he and his deputies were helpless. The embattled union officials, Hayes in tow, managed to fight their way into the Broadway theater, whence they escaped by the rear door, bruised and bleeding. The mob then surged on down the street to the Miner's Union Hall, which they proceeded to ransack. The union records were cast out of the second-story window to the street below. Furniture was splintered to pieces.

Alderman Frank Curran, a Socialist member of the city council and acting mayor, was foolish enough to climb to a second-story window in an attempt to reason with the mob. He was pushed out the window and in the fall broke an arm and sustained other injuries.

All day the riot continued. The safe was dragged from the building and dynamited. The police stood by but did not interfere. Far into the night, knots of rioters coursed up and down the streets of Butte looking for "Company men."

In the aftermath, the various factions had their explanations for what was obviously a planned and carefully executed riot. J. C. Lowney, executive board member of the W.F.M., who was present, was convinced that imported I.W.W.'s were responsible, that they feared a merger of the W.F.M. with the United Mine Workers of America and feared that such a consolidation would end their chances of taking over in Butte.

The *Montana Socialist* saw things differently. It remarked

that the cause was multiple, that it was part of a protest against "graft and abuse of official power" by the union officials; that those officials either were, or were supported by, "corporation agents"; that it was also a protest against the W.F.M. for overlooking abuses in the Butte local in return for the local's support of the W.F.M. The *Socialist* listed as further grievances: the rustling-card system, corporation espionage at union meetings, and political discrimination by Company agents against individual workers.

The trouble was far from over. The "progressives" immediately set about forming a new union. Unrecognized by Moyer and the W.F.M., they called a mass meeting and elected one Muckie McDonald president along with a slate of "progressive" officers. The charge was immediately leveled by the W.F.M. that the new union was I.W.W. controlled, a charge which McDonald emphatically denied.

On June 23, the Butte local of the W.F.M. held its regular meeting at the refurbished hall. A crowd gathered outside as darkness fell. Apparently as the crowd grew, the "progressives," now members of the new union, sensed trouble. They began to circulate in the crowd, counseling peace. Muckie McDonald rushed to the job-printing department of the Butte *Miner* and frantically had cards printed which read: "Fellow workers, in the name of your new union, keep peace and go home." No one went home.

The crowd grew, and men began to shout insults at the old union. In the midst of growing confusion, one Peter Bruno, a loyal W.F.M. man, pushed through the jostling bodies outside the door, attempting to get into the hall. A shot rang out, and Bruno fell dead on the sidewalk. Immediately there was a fusillade of shots from both inside and outside the building. One Ernest Noy was killed on the sidewalk across the street.

When the shooting started, the crowd dispersed. Within a short time the city was shaken by repeated dynamite blasts. Twenty-five separate blasts converted the Miner's Hall to rubble. The W.F.M. men had long since slipped out the back door and vanished in the night.

All that night, between the rocking blasts at the Union Hall, the sound of shots could be heard in the darkened city. The side streets were empty except for armed knots of men coursing back and forth looking for trouble. The sheriff was nowhere to be found; the police had locked themselves in the station house.

The next day the criminations and recriminations began again. Muckie McDonald said, "It was not done with our knowledge or consent. The Western Federationists started the whole thing." Moyer blamed the I.W.W.: "The wrecking crew of the I.W.W. is the force at work in Butte. . . . I have positive information that at least 600 I.W.W. agitators have arrived in Butte within the past week." The Company viewed the matter with Olympian objectivity. Its sentiment, expressed in the Butte *Miner*, was, "This is purely a squabble between miners' organizations in which other citizens have no part . . . it would be the part of wisdom for all persons to keep away from crowds. . . ."

At midnight on the night of the blasting, a worried governor, S. V. Stewart, was hanging on his telephone following developments at Butte. The next morning he announced his

Overleaf: Miners' Union Hall in Butte, dynamited in 1914. *Courtesy University of Montana Library.*

135

MINERS UNION HALL,

intention of sending troops to the city if the situation worsened. The governor was distraught not only because of the violence, but because he had an irate Moyer on his hands busily condemning not only the I.W.W., but Lewis J. Duncan, the Socialist mayor of Butte. Moyer believed that Duncan could have prevented the riot but deliberately did not choose to do so. Duncan, in turn, reported to the governor: "That a panicky state of mind exists here is beyond a doubt. . . . It looks to me as though the Anaconda Copper Mining Company were quite willing to have the new union completely destroyed."

The Company maintained silence. It did not ask for troops; it expressed no concern. It did shut down several of its mines. Violence, fights, and dynamiting continued throughout August. In late August the office of the Company's Parrot mine was blown up.

On September 1, 1914, Butte was placed under martial law because of the "existing lawlessness and defiance of authority," and the National Guard moved in. On September 9 the Company announced an open shop and said that henceforth it would neither deal with nor recognize any union. Its announcement was quietly righteous. From 1914 until June of 1917 there were no miners' organizations in Butte at all. In 1917 the International Union of Mine, Mill and Smelter Workers, an affiliate of the A.F. of L., came into Butte and began a laborious growth marked by violence and strife. The Company recognized no union in Butte until 1934.

The W.F.M. had failed; the new union had failed; the I.W.W. had failed (though it was not finished as yet), leaving the Company alone and victorious in the field.

VI. PANIC:
THE EARLY WAR YEARS

> In peaceable and quiet times, our legal rights
> are in little danger of being overborne; but when
> the wave of power lashes itself into violence and
> rage, and goes surging up against the barriers which
> were made to confine it, then we need the whole
> strength of an unbroken constitution to save us
> from destruction.
>
> Jeremiah Black, *Exparte* Milligan

THE foolishness began on the day that America entered the war, April 6, 1917. At first, sober-minded Montanans believed that it would pass, that the sudden release of long-pent passions had resulted in momentary aberration. It did not pass and it ceased to be mere foolishness. Before the war was over, hysteria had solidified into one of the most implacable attacks on civil liberties in the history of the country. That Montana should have been in the vanguard of America's loss of sense and judgment is a commentary in complexity.

The federal Sedition Act, which an embarrassed Congress repealed in 1921, was, in fact, patterned almost word for word on the Montana Sedition Act of 1918. No state in the Union engaged in quite the same orgy of book burning, inquisitions of suspected traitors, and general hysteria. Hundreds of suspects were hauled before Montana's Council of Defense to answer charges based on the rankest kind of rumor. County Councils of Defense were equally guilty of persecution; the courts jailed hundreds of "suspects" on the flimsiest of hearsay evidence; the press threw reportorial and editorial integrity to the winds and literally tried and convicted innocent Montanans in its pages.

Liberty Committees were organized in practically all the small towns of the state and became the local arbiters of patriotism. Billings even boasted a "Third Degree Committee," whose function was to round up and punish "financial slackers" and "pro-Germans." Anyone with a foreign accent was automatically suspected. People of German extraction were hounded and often found it completely impossible to demonstrate their loyalty. It was not sufficient to "kiss the flag" in public and to present receipts for contributions to the Red Cross, nor even to show a sheaf of Liberty Bonds.

Nor were Germans alone suspect; the Finns, the Irish, and the "Polacks" all came under the red, white, and blue scrutiny of self-appointed patriots. Letters from neighbors testifying to the "suspicious" activities of other neighbors flooded into the state and county Councils of Defense. The state Council of Defense, in particular, urged upon all Montanans that they watch their neighbors and report at once any "suspicious activity" or lack of enthusiasm for the war effort.

It all had its bizarre and ludicrous, as well as its tragic, aspects. The press carried repeated reports of enemy aircraft over Montana. The United States District Attorney, Burton K. Wheeler, received so many reports of enemy airplanes operating out of a secret hideaway in the Bitterroot Valley that he was forced to send a special agent to ferret out the enemy. Wheeler later remarked, "Just how and why the German High Command expected to launch an invasion of the United States through western Montana, 6000 miles from Berlin, never made the slightest bit of sense to me, but the reports generated by this kind of emotion could not always be brushed aside."

Burton K. Wheeler, United States Senator, 1922–46. *Courtesy Montana Historical Society.*

German airships were frequently seen, according to the Helena *Independent,* and they were "always going south." The *Independent* continued, "Three months ago, two reputable women residing near Missoula said they saw a burning airship fall into the forest near Hamilton. The sheriff of Ravalli County investigated and came back looking very mysterious. What he learned, he probably told the Secret Service only. . . ."

The I.W.W. was immediately singled out as a subversive organization. "There is a strong suspicion abroad," the Butte *Miner* stated, "that this I.W.W. element is working hand in glove with secret German agents in this country in an effort to paralyze the great industries of this nation."

The Anaconda *Standard* said, "Vast sums of money have been provided by Germany to stir up trouble in all the copper camps of the West. . . . A large amount has been sent to Butte. Who has the money?" The *Standard* offered the answer: the I.W.W., of course. Yet, of the 15,000 miners in Butte, the U.S. District Attorney estimated that fewer than 500 were I.W.W.'s, and this at the very height of I.W.W. influence.

The "Wobblies" were further reported to be busily poisoning wells, sawing down orchards, and burning crops. Presumably, too, they intimidated boardinghouse proprietors, especially if they were women, into refusing to provide lunches for the miners. At one time a vicious and rapacious army of 3,500 I.W.W.'s was poised in northwestern Montana preparing to move southward, laying waste to the countryside as they proceeded.

Pressed on the north by the Hun-inspired Wobblies, the Helena *Independent* described the perilous situation in the south: "Are the Germans About to Bomb the Capital City?" asked Will Campbell, the editor. Apparently so, because the paper offered a hundred-dollar reward to anyone who could spot the Hun craft which had been circling the city. "Have they spies in the mountain fastnesses equipped with wireless station and aeroplanes? Do our enemies fly around over our high mountains where formerly only the shadow of the eagle swept?"

In Butte, where the alien population percentage was high, District Attorney Burton K. Wheeler found himself inundated with reports of spies and saboteurs. He was quickly able to ascertain that most of the reports were based on "feuds among neighbors who seized on the spy scare to try to settle old scores." But the pressure on Wheeler was soon to become unremitting. In retrospect he wrote, "I was confronted with mass hysteria over alleged spies and saboteurs, and it still saddens and angers me when I think about it."

Montanans might look back on the bizarre stories and remember the hysteria with good-humored embarrassment except for what happened day by day to their fellow citizens, and to the structure of government by law.

Worse, hysteria and the intense patriotism of the average Montanan were soon employed for political purposes with chilling cynicism, and the official and unofficial bodies whose function presumably was to aid the war effort put themselves at the service of politics. In many instances that view was conditioned or even dictated by the Anaconda Company.

Not surprisingly, it started in Butte. Since 1914, labor in Butte had been simmering with resentment and discontent. It had no channel of communication with the Company except for Company-controlled "grievance committees." Not only did the rustling-card system exacerbate the suspicions of a chronically discontented labor force, the war led to increased pressures. Copper, lead, and zinc were vital to the

143

war effort, and as the prices of these metals increased, the Company increased production. The cost of living rose sharply, but wages did not. Working conditions, which had long been minimal, grew worse in the face of the accelerated mining activity. To this tinder of discontent, a large immigrant population added its opposition to the war. Two months after the declaration of war, the Pearce-Connally Club, an intransigent group of Irish, led a parade down the main street of the city carrying a huge red flag bearing the inscription, "Down With War."

On June 8, 1917, a fire broke out in the Speculator mine—a non-Company mine. Within minutes, flames and superheated fumes boiled up to the surface from the 2,400-foot level. Flames shot out from the surface "like a mighty geyser." Men in the "cage," which appeared at the surface along with the flames, were cremated before the horrified eyes of the surface crew.

As word of the disaster spread, a great crowd appeared at the Speculator. Rescue crews and machinery were rushed from as far away as Red Lodge, Montana, and Colorado Springs, Colorado, in an attempt to reach trapped miners. The heat was too intense to permit rescue operations.

Hour after hour the silent crowd stood watching and waiting. They did not move when the fire died away and the rescue crews were let down the shaft; they did not disperse when all of the 162 charred bodies had been brought to the surface. Many of the dead miners had been found piled against cement bulkheads, their fingers worn to the bone. The miners in the crowd knew perfectly well that state law required metal bulkheads which could be opened, and they knew that the law had never been enforced in Butte.

The Speculator disaster set off a strike and a sustained roar of anguish and anger in Butte. The Company's Butte *Post* responded to the disaster first with a grisly story entitled "Ghastly Sight at Morgue," but no story concerning the disaster *per se*, its cause, or steps which might be taken to prevent such disasters in the future. Concerning the strike, it ran a comment in the name of Anaconda and seven independent mines on the front page:

> No grievance of the workers in the Butte mines has been brought to the attention of the operators, and we believe that none exists. . . . The working conditions in the Butte area are better than the average and compare favorably with those of any other camp. . . . The miners of Butte will not permit a comparatively small band of cowardly agitators and non-workers to deprive them of their livelihood and drive them from their homes, but such protection as they require will be furnished them

Elsewhere, in response to a strike bulletin which had called working conditions in Butte "intolerable," the *Post* asserted that this attitude "reflects the Socialist-I.W.W. animus and purpose" and predicted that "responsible, intelligent, right minded citizens in this district, wage workers or business men, are not the advocates of summary methods . . . that might mean loss and involve the possibility of outright disaster for all concerned."

The strike which the Speculator disaster precipitated was spontaneous and represented a welling up of anger which had grown steadily since 1914. There was an immediate polarization. The Company attacked the strikers as I.W.W.'s and traitors and turned its press over to a violent excoriation of unpatriotic, Socialist "radicals," while labor, for the first time since 1914, sought to gain its ends through a union.

Three days after the disaster, the Metal Mine Workers

145

Union was formed. It presented a list of demands which, it said, if not met by June 15, would result in a general strike. The demands were straightforward: first, recognition of the Metal Mine Workers Union as the bargaining agent for all miners; abolition of the rustling-card system and of blacklisting; strict observance of the state mining laws; discharge of the state mine inspector; a wage increase; the right of free speech and assemblage.

The demands were peremptorily rejected by the Company. By June 29 more than 15,000 men were on strike in Butte, Anaconda, and Great Falls. The only voice the miners had consisted of the Butte *Bulletin*, which originated simply as a strike bulletin, but, edited by the brilliant and caustic W. F. Dunne, soon evolved into a radical labor paper. Its circulation, however, was small. The Company had not only its own press, but the sympathy of practically all the papers of the state which accepted the Company line that the miners had no real grievance and that the strike was I.W.W.-instigated, was grossly unpatriotic, sustained by funds supplied by "disloyal elements." Few Montanans read or heard the other side.

The anger of the strikers was rooted not only in the Speculator disaster and the rustling card, but also in working conditions which were, indeed, "intolerable." In June of 1917 the miners were paid $4.75 per day by an agreement which had been worked out in 1915. This scale was dependent on a 27-cent market price per pound of copper. This wage was to be raised if copper sold above 31 cents per pound. In the month of June, 1917, copper was selling at 32.5 cents; it had been above 31 cents since February, and had even reached 36.3 cents in March—yet there had been no increase in wages. The strikers were now asking for a flat $6 a day.

146

Wages in Butte *had* risen between 1914 and 1917. From an average wage of $894 per year (and a maximum of $1,050) in 1914, wages had risen to an average of $1,215 (and a maximum of $1,400) by 1917. But according to a study done for the Department of Labor as a consequence of the strife in Butte, the minimum subsistence level for a family of four in 1914 was $878, and the minimum "comfort" level was $1,108. By 1917, these figures had risen to $1,106 and $1,413 respectively. So the Butte miner was paid just enough to remain above subsistence level, but not enough to reach the level of comfort.

Again, the Department of Labor's study revealed that 80 per cent of the wage earners of Butte were in debt and that, in comparison with other mining camps, Butte's cost of living was higher, its wages lower than almost anywhere in the country.

As for safety conditions, on October 16, 1915, seventeen men had been killed in a mine accident, on February 14, 1916, twenty-one men had been killed, and statistics covering the three-year period from 1910 to 1913 for Company mines only, reveal that 5,795 miners suffered lost time due to injuries, and 162 were killed.

In 1917 and 1918, the U.S. Public Health Service estimated on the basis of a Butte study that due largely to poor ventilation and to working in "stagnant, hot, humid, and vitiated air, . . . at least 20 per cent of the underground workers who had been employed five years or more in the Butte mines had miners' consumption." No real effort to solve this problem had been made, and the miners on strike in 1917 knew it. Yet it was technically and economically feasible to solve the problem even then.

The U.S. Bureau of Mines also investigated the Butte sit-

147

uation in 1917 and 1918. Their report concluded that in 55 per cent of all the underground places where men were working, "There was absolutely no movement of air, and in an additional 18.3 per cent, the movement was slight." The report concluded, "It can readily be seen, therefore, that fumes from explosives may be considered dangerous to both health and life. . . ."

Yet the Company's Butte *Post* trumpeted early in the strike that wages in Butte were "the highest paid anywhere in the world" and Butte's living conditions were "very much superior to those of any other camp's. . . ." and the safety record "was gratifying, since fatalities are praiseworthily small."

Few Montanans exhibited any sympathy for the strikers. On June 14 the companies refused to meet with the union. The union had pledged that it would initiate no violence and denied that it was an affiliate of the I.W.W. The strike took place on schedule and 15,000 men were out by late June. The press began a steady drumfire of criticism. The Butte *Miner* joined the *Post* in calling for action. The solution, said the *Miner*, was ". . . to round up all the ringleaders who preached treason and hatred of the flag, and incarcerate them. . . ."

The Company, which had first used Pinkerton detectives in 1914, now imported not only Pinkertons but squads from the Thiel and Burns agencies. By late July there were more than two hundred detectives in Butte—nearly as many detectives as I.W.W.'s. Their fundamental assignment was to harass strike leaders, to work their way into the union and to report to the Company. To labor they were "goons" who formed "goon squads." They were widely feared.

At 3:00 A.M. on August 1, a black car drew up at 316 North Wyoming Street and discharged six masked men. They entered a boardinghouse there run by Mrs. Nora Byrne and asked for the room of one Frank Little. Informed that he was in room thirty-two, they ran swiftly to that room and kicked in the door. They dragged Little, still in his underwear, past a terrified Mrs. Byrne, hustled him into the car and roared away in the night. A few blocks away, the car stopped. Little was hauled roughly out, tied to the rear bumper, and dragged for several blocks. His kneecaps were scraped off.

He was again shoved into the car, which then sped to the Milwaukee bridge, a short distance outside the city limits, where he was hanged. When his body was discovered the next morning, there was a placard pinned to his underwear which bore the inscription: "Others take notice, first and last warning, 3-7-77." The numerals were the sign used by the early Montana vigilantes.

Little was a bona fide I.W.W. He had been chairman of the General Executive Board and had been an active I.W.W. organizer and agitator since 1906. He had come to Butte on July 18, 1917, and had immediately set about bolstering the strike, which had begun to falter with several hundred men returning to work.

The day after his arrival he spoke at the Butte ballpark at an open meeting of the Metal Mine Workers Union. There he reputedly called U.S. soldiers "uniformed scabs" and, with what the Butte *Miner* called "maniacal fury," he ". . . denounced the capitalists of every class and nationality. . . . He boasted of the fact that the present-day world-wide conflict meant nothing to him."

Thereafter, Little spoke wherever and whenever he could

Overleaf: The old mining town of Pardee. *Courtesy University of Montana Library.*

and quickly attracted the attention of the press. Since the Company had spies in the union as well as in the I.W.W., Little's actions were quickly brought to the attention of Company officials. His main theme at a meeting of the Metal Mine Workers Union was to convince the union that they must force those who had returned to work to quit. This was dutifully reported by a Company spy named Carl Dilling.

The Anaconda Company was not alone in its concern about Little. The few independent companies on the hill were also receiving detailed reports of his agitations. But the Anaconda Company, as always, took the leadership. L. O. Evans, chief counsel, C. F. Kelley (subsequently to become president), and John Gillie went to see U.S. District Attorney Wheeler about the matter. They disliked Wheeler, whom they considered to be a radical in sympathy with labor, but they disliked Little more. There were several conversations. Wheeler in due course took a copy of the federal Espionage Act of 1917 to Evans and asked him to point out under what section he could prosecute Little. Evans' only reply was that other district attorneys in other parts of the country seemed to be able to prosecute, why couldn't Wheeler?

On July 28, Little made another public speech. By this time the press had whipped itself into a frenzy. The *Post* headlined:

> In A Treasonable Tirade
> Little Says Constitution
> Is Mere Scrap of Paper

The *Post* followed a long story with the question: "How long is it [the community] going to stand for the seditious talk of this I.W.W. agitator whose traitorous words and appeals to violence addressed last night to a Butte audience are quoted in today's *Post*?" The answer, of course, came three days later with the lynching of Little.

Little's death resulted in immediate and long-range repercussions, both locally and nationally. The immediate press reaction was a tongue-clucking disapproval of lynch methods; but, as the Butte *Miner* put it, "As far as the man himself is concerned, his death is no loss to the world. . . ."

Will Campbell, editor of the Helena *Independent*, whose reputation for venom and vitriol was already well established, editorialized that one comment was heard everywhere: "Good work: Let them continue to hang every I.W.W. in the state" —and he added, "It sort of quickens the blood in the veins of some of the pioneers of Helena to see the fatal figures in print—3-7-77." Campbell, whose concomitant role as an inquisitor on the Montana Council of Defense was to form a black picture of bigotry and intolerance, wrote that Butte "disgraced itself like a gentleman" and he took to task the editors of other papers who disapproved of lynching. He called them "hypocritical" and "sentimental." "Tell the truth," he wrote, "If you are glad one of the troublemakers has paid the penalty of his acts, say so or keep still. You do not fool anyone by mouthing around over how sorry you are . . . you are absolutely satisfied with the work of the vigilance committees."

The radical Butte *Bulletin* bore the headline, "Frank Little Murdered by Gunmen, Companies in Desperation Resort to Deadly Violence." The *Bulletin* went on to announce that it had "sufficient evidence to indicate the names of five of the men who took part, every one of whom is a company stool pigeon. . . . Every man, woman and child in this county knows that Company agents perpetrated this foulest of all crimes." But the coroner's jury, when it met, declared Little to have been killed by "persons unknown." The crime was never solved.

Burton K. Wheeler was enraged. He issued a statement in which he said the lynching "is a damnable outrage, a blot on the state and county. . . . Every good citizen should condemn this mob spirit as unpatriotic, lawless and inhuman. . . . It is the worst thing that could have occurred to prevent a settlement of the labor troubles here."

In that analysis, Wheeler was quite correct. The murder intensified the hysteria which the press fueled continually. Will Campbell and the Helena *Independent* led the hue and cry. Campbell predicted a reign of terror as revenge for the murder. Mysterious German airplanes circling over Helena were now replaced by Arizona Apaches, who, incited by the I.W.W., were on the warpath again. The call for a special session of the legislature to pass a sedition act appeared in practically all the daily papers.

Montana's senator, Henry L. Myers, inundated with panicky reports from Montana, reported to Assistant Attorney General William Fitts that the situation was "truly alarming." Thirteen days after the murder of Little, Myers introduced an anti-sedition bill in the U.S. Congress. In support of his bill, Myers provided his colleagues with a copy of Will Campbell's editorial of August 19, 1917, and he described the Helena *Independent* as a "highly reputable and independent daily newspaper." The editorial in question was a typical Campbell diatribe, composed in equal parts of rumor and half truths. But Myers emphasized that Campbell was "in a position to speak advisedly and disinterestedly" about the situation.

The Myers bill was initially buried in the Judiciary Committee, but in an oddly juxtaposed series of events was picked up by the special session of the Montana Legislature and passed as the Montana Sedition Law on February 22, 1918. The same bill was then resurrected from the Judiciary Committee by Senator Thomas Walsh of Montana and became the federal Sedition Act on May 16, 1918.

Thus a federal law which was probably more restrictive of traditional American freedoms than any legislation since the Alien and Sedition Acts of 1798 was directly traceable to violence and conflict in Montana and the lynching of an I.W.W. agitator in Butte.

At least it may be said of the Congress that the debate on the issue was prolonged and that the opposition presented cogent arguments against the passage of legislation which arose from hysteria. The special session of the Montana Legislature which had passed the same law earlier was characterized by no such debate. Moreover, the special session went further and also passed a Criminal Syndicalism Law. The two laws made it a penal offense for any person to write or speak against the war or conscription. They made no distinction between those who opposed the war on principle and those who actually threatened national security. Sedition was punishable by a fine of not more than $20,000 or imprisonment for not more than twenty years and was defined as follows:

> Any person or persons who shall utter, print, write or publish any disloyal, profane, violent, scurrilous, contemptuous, slurring or abusive language about the form of government of the United States, or the Constitution of the United States, or the soldiers or sailors of the United States, or the flag of the United States, or the uniform of the army or navy of the United States, or any language calculated to bring the form of government of the United States . . . into contempt, scorn, contumely or disrepute, or shall utter, print, write or publish any

155

language calculated to incite or inflame resistance to any duly constituted Federal or *State authority* [italics mine] . . . shall be guilty of the crime of sedition.

The passage of the Montana Sedition Act and the Criminal Syndicalism Act not only outlawed the I.W.W., it rendered labor agitation of any effective sort a most dangerous activity. The Company's *Anaconda Standard* made the point in interpreting the legislation thus:

> There is no freedom of speech any longer for the disloyal or the pro-Germans. A man can talk all he pleases if he talks right. . . . The loyal people of this country have and will have all the freedom of speech and freedom of press they want. For the disloyal free expressions are over. Nor is it sufficient that one may claim that his disloyal expressions are his honest sentiments and that he is merely giving utterance to what he believes to be the truth. The man with disloyal sentiments must keep them to himself or take his punishment.

The murder of Frank Little not only marked the beginning of the end for the I.W.W., its violent aftermath brought federal troops to Butte and the strike sputtered out. The issues which had led to the walkout of 15,000 miners had been totally eclipsed by a press campaign focusing on disloyalty, spies, and sabotage. The Metal Mine Workers Union, like the W.F.M., and the "new union" before it, began to wither. The Company kept its open shop; it made no gestures toward improving conditions in the mines. Indeed, the fact of the existence of the I.W.W., however small the contingent in Butte, had been enormously helpful to the Company. It could, and did, equate any and all labor agitation, even in the face of the Speculator disaster, with the I.W.W. and hence with disloyalty.

Butte had a habit of occupying center stage, which, in this

instance, explains the eclipse of contemporaneous agitation elsewhere in Montana. Even as the city was crackling with tension over the murder of Frank Little, Montana's harried senior senator, Henry L. Myers, received a wire in Washington from five very important constituents in Missoula to the effect that the Industrial Workers of the World were threatening the property and lives of all the decent citizens of western Montana. "They are insulting the flag, belittling the authority of the government and are increasing in numbers. For weeks they have terrorized the lumber camps."

One of the signatories of the wire was Kenneth Ross, manager of the Anaconda's giant lumber operation in the West; another was C. H. McLeod, president of the Missoula Mercantile Company; and a third was Martin J. Hutchens, editor of the *Daily Missoulian*. What the Missoulians wanted was the immediate dispatch of federal troops "to disperse or arrest these . . . traitors."

The "trouble" was the most widespread lumber strike the country had ever seen. It began at Eureka, Montana, and spread rapidly to the Pacific Coast. Like the great strike in Butte, the trouble in the West was immediately attributed to the I.W.W. and to "disloyal elements." As in Butte, however, there was much more to it than that.

By 1917, the Northern Pacific Railroad and the Anaconda Company plus a handful of smaller operators, owned roughly 80 per cent of the timber in western Montana. The lumber industry was highly unstable. Just prior to the war the entire industry in the Pacific Northwest had suffered a four-year depression. Since labor represented the highest cost to the

Overleaf: Anaconda Company sawmill and facilities in Bonner, about 1910. *Courtesy University of Montana Library.*

operator, wages were poor, employment was sporadic, and working conditions were appalling. The labor force was migratory and the turnover was large. Small mills (about 150 in Montana) worked on contract with the Anaconda and Northern Pacific and these marginal operators in particular paid minimal wages for long hours. The lumberjack not only averaged a ten-hour day, he walked to and from the cutting area, even in below-zero weather. He was crammed into bunkhouses, forty or more to a unit. He slept two to a wooden bunk on a layer of straw. The district forester at Missoula described conditions in 1917 thus: "They have been treated not quite as good as workhorses, for usually there was more ventilation in the barns than in the bunkhouses. A 'get-the-hell-out-of-here' philosophy was to a great extent in vogue when any of the men complained about conditions."

The Montana labor commissioner, accompanied by a representative of the Board of Health, toured the Montana lumber camps in 1917 and reported that employers ". . . pay little attention to the comfort of employees and to sanitary conditions in the camps." The commissioner concluded, ". . . the forests of Montana are anything but a playground for those who follow the calling of a timberman," and he noted that "lumber companies seem to look upon every form of unionism with disfavor and aversion."

The strike that erupted in August of 1917 was rooted in long-standing resentment and discontent. Union organizers and agitators had been summarily fired, and it was not unusual for an entire crew to be laid off for "agitating." The strikers of 1917 wanted essentially what the Butte miners wanted: increased wages, no work on holidays and Sundays; better sanitation; better food; no more than twelve loggers to a bunkhouse; single beds with springs; shower baths and

Felling a tree with axes near Radnor. *Photograph by K. D. Swan, U.S. Forest Service, courtesy University of Montana Library.*

Skidding logs with high wheels. *Courtesy University of Montana Library.*

drying rooms; adequate lighting; and an eight-hour day. The lumber companies rejected the demands and refused to negotiate with committees appointed by the strikers. Although, again, the I.W.W. represented a minority of the strikers, the companies considered all strikers "disloyal." The secretary of the Montana Lumberman's Association wrote to Governor S. V. Stewart that these "enemy agents" were misleading and deceiving the loggers. He accused them of polluting wells, letting cockroaches loose in cookhouses, breaking shovel handles, planting lice in bunkhouses, putting calomel in the food, and crippling horses in the feed stables.

The lumber strike petered out like the copper strike. Federal troops acted as strikebreakers in Whitefish and Columbia Falls, and, surprisingly, individual lumbering concerns made concessions to groups of loggers. The one difference between the strike in Butte and in the woods camps lay in this fact. Oddly enough, it was the Anaconda Company that assumed leadership in this strategy. At a meeting of the Montana Lumber Manufacturers Association in Missoula on September 15, 1917, Kenneth Ross argued for a concerted campaign involving the installation of bathing facilities, steel bunks and springs, reading facilities, and standardized menus. It took six hours to win the endorsement of the association, but the operators finally went on record with their approval. The subsequent history of labor problems in the woods versus the mines points up the tragedy of the failure of the mine operators to listen to the legitimate complaints of the workers as the lumbermen ultimately did. Concessions by the lumber companies led to sustained peace in the woods; the failure of the mining companies to concede even minimally resulted in a half century of conflict.

By the middle of the unusually cold and brittle winter of

1917, the rebellion of labor in Montana was over. Federal troops stood by wherever needed. On every issue and at every turn, the Company, its press, and its allies had won. The control was tight. Call it patriotism or power, the corporate view of rectitude and the proper order of things prevailed. Yet there were Montanans who had watched it all with misgivings and a growing sense of outrage. They were beginning to speak up—and so the contest moved from the woods and the mines into the political arena.

VII. THE INQUISITION

A cloud has arisen upon Montana's horizon that threatens dire consequences to the people of the state. Class is being arranged against class and bitterness is being engendered; and if the lawlessness cited is not put down, and the right of free speech is not rescued from the disrepute thrown upon it, in my opinion, conditions may follow that will do the people and the fair name of the state incalculable injury.

From a letter to the Montana Council of Defense, 1918, from Attorney General Sam C. Ford.

FEDERAL District Judge George M. Bourquin was a crusty man. Contemporaries described him as "vain," "arrogant," and "irascible." "He was," wrote B. K. Wheeler, "what some of us used to call a 'slave driver.'" Young attorneys, in particular, dreaded trying a case before him; experienced attorneys approached him with caution and deference. His written decisions, replete with references to the classics, were studies in rolling, Victorian prose.

He had few intimate friends. When he was presiding over a case, he refused to eat with anyone and invariably asked the waitress to tip up the other chairs around his table in order to discourage intimacy.

He was also unorthodox. He exasperated lawyers and litigants alike by addressing himself directly to the jury and instructing them as to their findings. He often fixed a baleful eye on the jury and, in effect, demanded a certain verdict. He did this on one occasion when the defendant was charged with a minor liquor violation. Bourquin instructed the jury to find the man innocent, which they did. Turning to the de-

167

fendant, Bourquin said, "The court finds you not guilty"—
and as the man turned to leave the courtroom, he added,
"And don't do it again." He was fond of repeating, "This
court may be wrong, but not in doubt."

It was before this judge that an increasing flood of cases
were tried involving "slackers," I.W.W.'s, and those charged
with violation of the original federal Sedition Act of 1917.
Controversy and an increasing hostility swirled around him
as, in case after case, he found the defendants innocent or dismissed the cases for lack of evidence before they came to
trial. "By some fatal coincidence," wrote the chairman of the
Butte draft board, "[this man] is presiding over this very
Federal District where relentless and certain punishment of
evasion of the duties of citizenship is a paramount necessity."
The press soon joined the critics, particularly Will Campbell's Helena *Independent*. Campbell even went so far as to
write Montana's Senator H. L. Myers, "There is going to be
trouble, deep, wide and serious, and don't you forget it. . . .
Men are determined to rid the state of Wobblies, slackers,
disloyalists and traitors. . . ," and he demanded that Myers
have Bourquin removed from the state for the duration of
the war.

Guy E. LaFollette, managing editor of the *Independent*,
wrote the United States Attorney General and flatly accused
Bourquin of being pro-German. Bourquin, he wrote, came
from Butte, whose spies and propagandists had influenced
him. He had become even worse, said LaFollette, since his
son had been drafted. Impeachment was too long a process,
and death was not likely since Bourquin was "an exceedingly
healthy specimen of whatever he is. . . . But," he added,
"Montana is fed up with Bourquin," and he, too, suggested
transferring the judge to another district.

If Bourquin was aware of the growing animosity toward him, he gave no sign. The federal court term in July, 1917, witnessed seventy informations filed for failing to register for the draft. Bourquin sentenced thirty-six to one day in jail and gave the remainder thirty- to sixty-day sentences. During the same court term he dismissed the conspiracy charges against the leaders of the Pearce-Connally Club. He said, in rendering the opinion, "Rights must be protected by the courts at all times but more zealously at a time like this . . . when passions are more or less aroused." To beleaguered U.S. District Attorney Wheeler, Bourquin said, "Send some of those sedition cases up to me and I'll take care of them. I am in a stronger position than you are."

It was, however, the Ves Hall case that brought the wrath of nearly every Montanan down upon Bourquin's head. Hall was a rancher from Rosebud County, and he was arrested for uttering alleged "seditious remarks." He was accused of having said that the Germans had a right to sink the *Lusitania* because it was carrying munitions, that the war was a Wall Street millionaire's war, that America had no business being in it. The case came to trial before Bourquin in January, 1918; the charge was that Hall had violated the federal Sedition Act of 1917.

Wheeler was absent from the state, and the prosecution was conducted by his assistant, Homer G. Murphy, on the basis of the fact that Hall had violated section three of the act in that he did "make and convey false reports and false statements with intent to interfere with the operation and success of the military and naval forces of the United States. . . ." Judge Bourquin granted defense attorney Matt Canning's motion for a directed verdict and found Hall innocent. At the same time, he dismissed an action involving the same charge against A. J. Just, an Ashland banker, who had made similar remarks.

Bourquin on this occasion explained his decision fully "to the end that a precedent be established." He found Hall's statements "unspeakable," but he found no evidence on which to base a verdict of guilty. The remarks were made in a remote Montana town with a population of some sixty people. The nearest railroad was sixty miles away with "none of the armies or navies within hundreds of miles." Hall had made some of the statements in obvious badinage. If, indeed, Hall had deliberately intended to obstruct recruitment and enlistment services, that was not a crime under the act. Certainly the place and timing of the remarks gave no support to the contention that he intended to interfere with the military.

Slander, said Bourquin, should be punishable by law, but not under the federal Sedition Act—and he added, "Since the sedition law had its share in the overthrow of the Federalists and the elevation of Jefferson to the Presidency and his party to power, Congress has not ventured to denounce as crimes, slanders and libels of government and its officers. The genius of democracy and the spirit of our people and times seem yet unable to avoid greater evils than benefits from laws to that end."

The Ves Hall decision raised havoc not only in Montana, but also in Washington. It prompted Montana's junior senator, Thomas Walsh, already smarting from the criticisms resulting from the lynching of Frank Little, to resurrect Senator Myers' sedition bill from the Judiciary Committee and introduce it as an amendment to the existent sedition act.

The Department of Justice, already burdened with a heavy volume of mail demanding the removal of B. K. Wheeler as U.S. district attorney, now felt intense pressure not only from Montana, but also from Montana's Congressional delegation, concerning Bourquin. The attorney general, Thomas W. Gregory, asked his assistant, John O'Brian, if Bourquin's decision could not be appealed. O'Brian studied the case and replied that he did not think so—and added gratuitously, "The record of his rulings in our files show unmistakably that the real trouble with him is that he is distinctly against the proper enforcement of any of the war statutes and is out of sympathy with their purpose."

Military intelligence was also concerned. Colonel F. G. Knabonshue, an intelligence officer in the Western Department, reported, "Judge Bourquin should be transferred and a man 500 per cent American sent to Butte . . . also, the reappointment of Mr. Wheeler [should be] killed."

The Justice Department, having just completed a preliminary investigation of Wheeler, concluded, "It is the view of this department that the responsibility for the unfortunate conditions in Montana rests not upon him [Wheeler] but upon the United States District Judge [Bourquin]."

Bourquin himself was fully aware that a directed verdict could not be appealed and that to try Hall again on the same charge would place him in double jeopardy. He was also aware of the agitation the case had aroused in Washington and in Montana. He went imperiously about his business, tipping up chairs in restaurants and walking alone in the streets of Butte and Helena. He was, indeed, almost completely sealed off by a wall of hostility.

Wheeler was also suffering. On a trip to Washington he made it a point to drop into the Department of Justice and call on Attorney General Gregory. Gregory assured him that he did not have to resign, but thought perhaps, in view of the circumstances, he would like a federal judgeship in Panama.

Wheeler retorted, "If you're going to deport me, you'd better make it Siberia."

Wheeler, too, suffered increasing ostracism. He later remarked, "People avoided me on the street and nudged one another to point me out in hotel lobbies, muttering threats I could overhear. . . . Friends warned me that I had better be more careful, lest some terrible violence be visited upon me." Wheeler's answer was that he was probably the safest man in Montana, because if anything happened to him people would immediately blame the Anaconda Company—which its officials well knew.

In retrospect, the Ves Hall decision was not only courageous, it was based on incontrovertible rectitude as far as law was concerned. In light of the specific stipulations of the Sedition Act of 1917, Bourquin could have come to no other decision. What Wheeler referred to as the "statutes-be-damned attitude which was second-guessing my every move" had had no effect on Bourquin. Yet paradoxically, or perhaps inevitably, the Ves Hall decision resulted, both locally and nationally, in a kind of victory for the super-patriots. It was fundamental in assuring the passage of the Montana Sedition Act of 1918; it was basic to the passage of the drastically restrictive federal Sedition Act, which was based on the Montana legislation, and it was in light of the decision that the Montana Legislature convened in special session three weeks later to engage in an orgy of patriotic expatiation.

Governor S. V. Stewart addressed the special session on February 14, 1918, with a speech calling for action to enact a law "here in Montana that will make available a mighty means of throttling the traitor and choking the traducer." He said that "Every disloyal utterance and every treasonable act is duly reported to the German people. . . . The tender mother is startled by the mere suggestion that [her] boy may not come back, the father clenches his fists at the very suspicion that any of his own acquaintances might conspire to encompass the destruction of his son and heir." In the Annals of State of the State messages, marked ordinarily in Montana by extraordinary pedestrianism, Stewart's address is remarkable for the high pitch of its frenzy and the admixture of tear-jerking sentimentality and violent references to "traitors in our midst," "poisoned tentacles," and "vipers circulating the propaganda of the junkers." He was confident that the special session would act to protect that "mother" so that she would not awaken to find that disloyalty had destroyed her boy and "that the timber of her manhood has decayed, that the luster of her womanhood is tarnished."

The session lost little time in passing the Sedition Act and the Criminal Syndicalism Act. Indeed, the assembly could have met, passed the two pieces of legislation unanimously, and adjourned in the space of three days—but there were other things to be done.

Joint resolutions calling for the resignations of Bourquin and Wheeler were introduced. The resolution concerning Bourquin was tabled, that concerning Wheeler was defeated by one vote. The Bourquin resolution did not get to the floor because, according to Wheeler, "[of] his reputation for dealing with any interference with the processes of his court through stiff contempt penalties," and "also, the mining companies had no desire to antagonize him because they had important claims cases pending before him."

Then the session turned its attention to Charles L. Crum, judge of the Fifteenth Judicial District of Montana. Judge Crum, from Rosebud County, had sent Ves Hall and A. J. Just to see Wheeler after their indictment to seek his advice.

Sam V. Stewart, Governor of Montana, 1917–21. *Courtesy University of Montana Library.*

174

He had further been a character witness for Ves Hall at his trial. The special session could not impeach Bourquin, and they could not remove Wheeler. Crum was another matter. By unanimous vote and for "disloyalty and pro-German sentiments," they impeached him. Wheeler later wrote, "I considered this a tragedy, for I thought Crum a fine and honorable man."

Next the session passed legislation making legal the extra-legal Montana Council of Defense. The council had existed since the early days of the war, but its actions had had no legislative sanction. Its members had been appointed by the governor, and it had immediately set about co-ordinating patriotic activities all over the state. It was hampered because it had no funds and, moreover, found it difficult to investigate cases of disloyalty, sabotage, and espionage without the power to subpoena, which could only be granted by the legislature. The final act of the special session of 1918 was formally to create the Montana Council of Defense and to endow it with extraordinary powers to "do and perform all acts and things necessary or proper so that the military, civil and industrial resources of the state may be most efficiently applied toward maintenance of the defense of the state and nation, and toward the successful prosecution of such war, and to that end, it shall have all the necessary power not herein specifically enumerated."

The legislature appropriated twenty-five thousand dollars for the council, until the next general session. Then, after eleven days of "deliberation," the special session adjourned, leaving in the hands of the Council of Defense the welfare and security of the state.

The original council had been formed in response to a general request from President Wilson that each state create such a body to function under the over-all direction of a Council of National Defense. Governor Stewart responded with alacrity and so effectively did the new council operate that within a month's time it had organized County Councils in all of Montana's forty-three counties. Because the state was so large and sparsely populated, the State Council went further and organized Community Councils on the basis of school districts and voting precincts. In theory, then, the Council of National Defense topped an organization which literally reached into the grass roots.

Prior to their "legalization" in the winter of 1918, the councils concentrated upon agricultural matters and upon assisting in the national campaign to increase agricultural production. Their second realm of activity was to assist in Liberty Bond drives. Montana's allotment for the first bond drive was $7,000,000; it raised $15,000,000. Its allotment for the second was $15,000,000 and it raised $20,000,000. The County Councils, in particular, were responsible for this accomplishment. A general increase of 30 per cent in agricultural production attested to the effectiveness of the council system in its agricultural role.

The State Council was also charged by the National Council with a responsibility for "military mobilization" and "recruitment," and it was via this charge that it first involved itself in the problem of "slackers" and "draft dodgers."

By the winter of 1917 the councils were so well organized and had performed so effectively that Montanans in all walks of life were turning to them for advice, aid—and with a variety of complaints and fears. As a consequence of the strikes in Butte and the western woods, and as the I.W.W. moved into the growing turmoil, the councils gave more and more of their attention to matters of loyalty, espionage, and sedition. Almost without exception, the County Councils were run by the most prestigious men in the community. They were appointed by the governor and, true to the governor's own leanings, most of the appointees were businessmen of long standing and of conservative convictions.

The State Council was deeply involved in, and frustrated by, the strikes, alleged espionage, disloyalty, and turmoil, prior to its reconstitution in February, 1918. Its lack of power, particularly in the face of the sustained press campaign, irked its members deeply.

The new council, appointed in the winter of 1918, carried over four of the seven appointees to the first council. Most active among them (and the most frustrated) was Will Campbell, editor of the Helena *Independent*, vice-president of the Montana Loyalty League, fiery zealot, and super-patriot.

To Campbell, no constitution, no court, no statute justified the obstruction of the war effort. His editorials in the *Independent* were unparalleled for venom. Even William Dunne, radical and caustic editor of the Butte *Bulletin*, paid him a backhanded tribute. When Dunne testified before the council, Campbell sarcastically asked him where he received his newspaper training. Dunne replied, ". . . principally through observation. After all, the Helena *Independent* is on our exchange list."

Other carry-overs on the new council were the secretary, Charles Greenfield, who had worked for Campbell on the *Independent* and had served in the legislature from 1909 to 1916. Like Governor Stewart himself, Greenfield was *ex officio*.

Charles J. Kelly was a Butte resident, president of the Daly Bank and Trust Company, an Anaconda Company-controlled bank, and he was also president and manager of the Hennesey Mercantile Company.

Mrs. Tyler B. Thompson had been president of the Montana Federation of Women's Clubs and represented the women of Montana. She rarely spoke and voted consistently with the majority.

New on the council as of 1918 (membership had been increased to eleven) were Newton T. Lease, formerly the mayor of Great Falls, former Republican legislator, now a large and successful contractor; Sidney M. Logan, formerly Republican mayor of Kalispell; Samuel Sansburn, prosperous farmer from Bloomfield; Charles Victor Peck, a rancher from Danvers and president of the Montana Loyalty League; Ignatius Daniel O'Donnell of Billings, farmer and director of the Mercantile National Bank; Mortimer M. Donoghue, a plumber from Butte and president of the conservative Montana Federation of Labor.

Of the eleven members of the council, Stewart, Campbell, and Greenfield were the most aggressive and verbose; Campbell, Peck, Logan, and Sansburn were all vice-presidents of the Montana Loyalty League, Danvers its president. Four members were Republican, three Democrats, and four billed themselves as nonpartisan.

The council also availed itself of advisers, some paid, some not. Prominent in this category were L. O. Evans, chief counsel for the Anaconda Company; J. Bruce Kremer, a Butte attorney with intimate Company connections; and John Brown, a Helena attorney whom the council ultimately retained to preside over its selection of books to be banned in public and school libraries.

The council's official legal adviser was Sam C. Ford, attorney general, but Ford's growing disapproval of its methods led it to seek counsel elsewhere, most notably from L. O. Evans and J. Bruce Kremer.

The council's first act was to grant itself investigatory powers under the broad legislative authority given it, including the power to subpoena. Witnesses could be represented by counsel and could be questioned by any member of the council.

The second order of business was to promulgate a series of "orders," the violation of which was to be punishable by not more than one year in jail or a fine not to exceed one thousand dollars. Order Number One, issued to prevent "riots, affrays, breaches of the peace and other forms of violence," made it illegal to conduct any "parade, procession, or other public demonstration, funerals excepted, on any of the streets, highways, or public places of the State of Montana without the written permission of the governor as *ex-officio* chairman of this council."

Order Number Two stated that vagrants, healthy beggars, "persons who roam about from place to place . . . every lewd and dissolute person . . . every common prostitute and common drunkard" be imprisoned for a period not to exceed ninety days. Feeling that this section should be "made broader and more comprehensive," the council further ordered that any person not engaged in some legitimate occupation for "five days stated each week" must register with the city clerk, county clerk, or justice of the peace, "setting forth the reason why he is not engaged in some legitimate occupation." By October 7, 1918, the council had issued seventeen orders. In seven months, by its "orders" it established the framework for an orderly, moral, proper, fervently patriotic, and rigidly orthodox Montana. The voluminous correspondence of the council, as well as the thick volumes of verbatim testimony, indicated that again and again in matters ranging from the appointment of County Council members to sabotage and spies, the council sought the advice of the Anaconda Company—and followed it.

It was inevitable that the council would summon B. K. Wheeler. By the spring of 1918 Wheeler had come to symbolize everything the council hated and feared. Bourquin was immune; Wheeler was not. Yet they could not subpoena him without some cause.

The door opened a little when the senior senator, Myers, sought the council's advice about the reappointment of Wheeler as district attorney. Stewart immediately polled the members and reported to Myers that to a man they opposed the reappointment.

Shortly thereafter, the State and County Councils met in joint session. Wheeler forthwith became the center of impassioned discussion. J. M. Kennedy, of the Libby Council, demanded that the State Council remove him. Told that the State Council did not have that power, Kennedy said, "This state is burning with patriotism. . . . I hope you will [remove Wheeler] even though it is not constitutional [applause]. . . . And so, sir, I sincerely hope that even though it is not, in the view of some of the constitutional lawyers of the state just exactly as my little friend Judge Fitzgerald used to say, *mal querelle pas*, let us do it anyway." Other speakers rose eagerly to condemn Wheeler and at the close of the session the council passed a resolution, to be sent to the President and the Senate of the United States, which concluded that the reappointment of Wheeler "would be inimical and injurious to the best interests of this State and the peace of its peoples." But they still had not had the opportunity to grill Wheeler himself.

That opportunity came as the result of a bizarre spy case in which Wheeler was involved. Oscar Rohn, president of the South Butte Mining Company, hired an alien, Carl von Pohl, to spy on the I.W.W. Von Pohl, who was a caricature of a spy, sporting a Van Dyke beard, and possessing a sinister visage and a thick accent, after reporting all manner of skulduggery and mysterious goings-on to Rohn, got himself arrested for making pro-German remarks—at which juncture Wheeler entered the case. Rohn, having hired a pro-German as a spy, was now accused of being pro-German and the Council of Defense summoned him to testify.

It was immediately apparent that the council had only a passing interest in Rohn. The "accused" was Burton K. Wheeler. The inquisition of Wheeler covers some one hundred pages of question-and-answer testimony in the records of the council.

Wheeler, aware that the council had already expressed its sentiments concerning his reappointment (although just prior to his testimony, the council rescinded its motion of censure in the light of Wheeler's imminent appearance), started his testimony by stating, "I have been told that the purpose of my coming here, and the purpose of subpoenaing me was for the purpose of trying me, so to speak. . . . The law, as I read it, provides that this council was organized for the purpose of assisting our office. . . . I don't fancy the idea of being subpoenaed over here in a summary fashion before your council."

Wheeler went on to accuse the council of already having sent resolutions to Washington and further accused Campbell of "nasty insinuations" in the *Independent* concerning his appearance before the council.

Reading between the lines of the testimony, one can almost

feel the palpable shock of the council, confronted at long last by its enemy, at the reversal of roles. Wheeler immediately took the initiative and the accusers became the accused. The council had become accustomed to frightened witnesses and obsequious answers. Now came Burton K. Wheeler, quite another kind of witness. Several members of the council knew him only by reputation; none knew him well, with the possible exception of Campbell, whom Wheeler had once prosecuted for contempt of court.

In later years many Montanans were to hear the flat, harsh voice lashing out at the establishment, and watch the stabbing finger and pale blue eyes as Wheeler drove his points home. He had no oratorical style, and he often scrambled his syntax, but the implacability in his voice, his stance, and his sharp gestures rendered his performance peculiarly effective. Nothing rattled him or threw him off base. His anger was all the more impressive for its cold containment.

Will Campbell began the inquisition. Waiting in reserve were the Anaconda Company's L. O. Evans and J. Bruce Kremer. Campbell accused Wheeler of complimenting William Dunne of the radical Butte *Bulletin* in a speech he had delivered in Great Falls: "Did you carry the idea in that address . . . that would leave the casual reader to believe the I.W.W. were much abused, you kind of referred to 'us'; they call 'us' I.W.W."

Wheeler shot back, "I said it, and I meant it," and he went on to assert that of the twelve thousand miners out in Butte, only about five hundred were I.W.W.'s. He asserted that there never would have been a strike had the miners been treated as they should have been.

N. T. Lease said to Wheeler, "You are aware of the fact that the verdict of the State of Montana, [that is] that if the federal officials of Butte had been doing their duty, that it would not have been necessary for the citizens of Butte to hang Mr. Little."

Wheeler snapped, "I don't agree that it [was] the verdict of the people of Montana. . . . Some people believe that . . . because of the fact that some of the newspapers in the state . . . have made the charge absolutely without foundation."

Will Campbell rose to the bait with a sarcastic remark to which Wheeler replied that the Helena *Independent* was "absolutely subsidized and subservient to the mining interests of the state."

Campbell retorted that Wheeler was a Socialist. Said Wheeler, "I am not a Socialist, never have been a Socialist and never expect to be a Socialist . . . [but] a great many of the principals [*sic*] of Socialism are correct, and they are being adopted by the Democratic and Republican parties."

At one juncture in the hearing, a completely frustrated L. O. Evans of the Company shouted, "In the prosecution of these aliens you did nothing! That's what I blame you for!" But, Wheeler persisted, you cannot prosecute on the basis of rumor, only on the basis of the law. "There is such a thing as a treasonable utterance in common parlance, but as matter of law there is treason, but there is not any such crime as treasonable utterance."

Campbell's questions became more and more personal. Had Wheeler contributed to the Liberty Bond drives? Had he contributed to the Red Cross? What war work had he done? What patriotic speeches had he made? The questions involved his income tax returns, his church affiliation, and, particularly, his friends. Were many of his friends not radicals, I.W.W.'s, Non-Partisan League members? Behind the questioning lay the constant implication of disloyalty.

Wheeler had the last word. He flatly accused the council of political motivation. He expressed contempt rather than anger for their lack of understanding of the law. He left the hearing with the council, particularly Campbell, simmering in their anger. They promptly reaffirmed their opposition to his reappointment and mailed the resolution to Washington.

In the long and dreary procession of frightened and confused witnesses who were hauled before the council, only William Dunne matched Wheeler's performance. Unlike Wheeler, Dunne was urbane, cool, and articulate. The *Bulletin*, radical, outspoken supporter of the I.W.W., bitter critic of the Anaconda Company, had been a thorn in the side of the mining interests and the council since its inception in 1917. Campbell, in particular, had been incensed when Dunne editorialized about the council's resolution on Wheeler. The resolution, said Dunne, would receive about as much attention as "a prohibition resolution at a Brewery Worker's Union." Dunne went on to say the members of the council "have grown lean and gray or fat and bald in the service of big business. All are tried and trusty lieutenants of the same old political gang. They are all birds of a feather, and they flock together at Helena, supposedly working for the state, but apparently for political reasons of their own."

Campbell was a power in the Association of Montana Newspaper Editors, and shortly after Dunne's editorial appeared, the association presented a file of the *Bulletin* to the council with the request that it investigate "the desirability of presenting these . . . to the proper postal authorities." The *Bulletin*, said the association, is "not in accord with the spirit of the times and [tends] to hinder and delay the war program . . . by creating dissension and prejudice at a time when loyalty and unity of purpose is earnestly sought."

184

William Dunne accordingly appeared before the council. If anything, he disturbed them more greatly than Wheeler. Asked what he meant by "in the service of big business," Dunne settled down and lectured the council on classical Marxism. Asked his view of Wheeler, he replied, "I don't mean to say that Mr. Wheeler is the millennium, but he is an improvement on most of the politicians of this state."

Dunne had repeatedly urged his readers to ignore the council since it was a joke and not legally constituted. When questioned about this he calmly replied that he intended to continue so advising his readers until the council's orders had been tested in the courts, that he considered the council not only illegal but foolish and motivated by antediluvian politics. He denied any affiliation with the I.W.W., but made no secret of his Marxist views. With that, Dunne was dismissed.

The matter did not end there. In September, 1918, another strike occurred in Butte. Cornelius F. Kelley, then vice-president of Anaconda, stated that he would never deal with the union. The *Bulletin*, true to form, castigated the Company and baited the federal troops that were still in the city. At the request of the County Council of Defense, the Butte police, aided by the troops, made a series of raids on suspected I.W.W.'s, which included the offices of the *Bulletin*. Dunne and the staff were arrested, hauled before the County Council, charged with sedition and turned over to the county attorney for prosecution. Legal gyrations ensued and the matter came before Judge Bourquin, who expressed his view of the initial raid thus: "There was no disorder save by the raiders. These armed [raiders] perpetrated an orgy of terror, violence and crime against citizens and aliens in public assemblage, whose only offense seems to have been peaceable insistence upon the exercise of a clear legal right."

Dunne was finally convicted of sedition by the local court in 1920 and was fined $5,000. The war, however, was over, and hysteria was on the wane. The Supreme Court reversed the decision.

If, in the cases of Wheeler and Dunne, the council suffered setbacks, its other activities were crowned with complete success. Its book-banning activities, directed by Helena attorney John Brown, were notably successful. Brown's interest was aroused when his child brought a book home from school by Professor Willis Mason West entitled *The Ancient World*. Brown was shocked to discover that in West's book "The great contributions to civilization in the West were Roman and *Teutonic*." In reporting his find to the State Council, Brown found the book to be "distinctly German propaganda." He was horrified to discover that it was used as a text in forty-two Montana high schools.

So impressed was the council with Brown's analysis that they hired him to probe other works in school libraries.

The council was somewhat nonplussed when West himself appeared to protest the ban and the publishers were agitated enough to issue a circular entitled "Pro German Attack on West's History." But though the council found that West himself was not disloyal, they banned the book nonetheless. Brown was so infuriated by the publisher's circular that he wrote to West calling the author of the circular "an unmitigated, damnable liar."

Order Number Three banned not only West's history, but, based on Brown's findings, it also instructed all libraries to destroy the following books:

> Pope, *Writing and Speaking German*
> Betz, *About the Great King and Other Things*

Hohfeld, *German Song Book*
Manley, *A Summer in Germany*
Dirk, *German Songs*
Krause, *First German Reader*
Pope, *German Compositions*
Harris, *Selections for German Compositions*

Order Number Three further stated that all librarians were to examine their books and eliminate any which seemed "to contain German propaganda."

Attorney Brown went into a paroxysm of letter writing, inquiries, and studies of books. To the few who disagreed with his judgment as to what was or was not propaganda, he fired off stern letters. To a teacher in Brockway who questioned his judgment of West's text, he wrote: "Your undated, misspelled and poorly written letter to the State Council of Defense has been transmitted to me. . . . You show a lack of knowledge of your own American history, otherwise you would well remember the remarkable words of Washington, when he calls attention to the need of obedience to constituted authority. . . . Your letter is astonishing to me. . . . [It] confirms the ignorance that is behind it."

But for the most part, Brown basked in enthusiastic letters of compliance. Another teacher from Brockway reported triumphantly that she had "weeded out all German texts, clipped out all German words and clipped out all German songs in our books of national songs, blotted out German flags in the dictionaries." She added with consummate righteousness, ". . . and we also spell germany without a capital letter." Brown's file was soon thick with similar letters.

Order Number Three also forbade the use of the German

187

language anywhere and at any time, and this section of the order led to a long procession of frightened violators, including ministers, many of whom had congregations which understood only German. A Lutheran minister from Laurel, where there was a large German population, appeared to beg for reconsideration since his service would be incomprehensible in English. His request was refused.

One minister, the Reverend F. E. Brauer of Dooley, pled for just one service in German and accompanied his plea with statistics concerning the loyalty of his congregation—$1,385 worth of war stamps, all members of the Red Cross, all buyers of war bonds. His request was refused.

This section of Order Number Three led to a mass exodus of Mennonites from Montana to Canada—an exodus marked by great hardship and economic loss. There were some seven hundred families located in Chinook County, all of whom were involved. E. C. Leedy, of the Immigration Department of the Northern Pacific Railroad wrote to the council, ". . . these German Mennonites . . . are among our best farmers, and we would dislike very much to see them leave the country."

Secretary Greenfield answered Leedy's letter stating that the Mennonites had gotten their land free from "Uncle Sam" (which was not the case), and said, "Your Mennonites appear to be under the impression that they can only worship God in the German language. They are so dense . . . they are willing to move. . . . I think it just as well that Montana and all other states lose a class of people who are so selfish and as absolutely self centered and as lacking in love of country as these Mennonites. . . ." Order Number Three stood, and the Mennonites left the country. Secretary Greenfield expressed the complete satisfaction of the council, and particularly his own satisfaction, at this purging of ungrateful peoples.

If the State Council's activities were crowned with success, the County Councils were even more successful. They, after all, were literally at the grass roots. They were given the same powers as the State Council by order of that body, subject only to review by the State Council. Like the State Council, they turned their efforts solely toward investigation after February, 1918. Often they worked closely with local units of the Montana Loyalty League or local Liberty Committees.

In practically every county of the state, the councils put in long and arduous hours listening to testimony from those accused of disloyalty—of being slackers, of not supporting Liberty Loan drives. The loan drives represented peaks in the activity of the County Councils. One local advertisement read, "No mercy for bond shirkers"; another, "A bond shirker is an enemy to humanity and liberty, a traitor and a disgrace to his country." Several councils threatened to publish the names of all non-contributors in the local newspaper.

In Ravalli County, the council called a farmer named Victor E. Brown in an interrogation concerning his failure to contribute to a bond drive. His answers revealed that he was deeply in debt and on the edge of bankruptcy.

Question: You say you have not contributed further other than your wife and you are members of the Red Cross?

Answer: Yes, sir.

Question: It is your intention to buy War Savings Stamps or contribute anything toward the War Service League?

Answer: We are very glad to when we see ourselves clear.

Question: In other words you don't feel you are able to do it until you pay all your debts.

Answer: Not all of our debts; we deny ourselves a great many things we would like to have. We are living in a wreck of a house. The improvements on that place are in bad condition.

Question: In other words you are looking toward your own comfort all the time?

The voluminous records which the County Councils sent to the State Council are appalling evidence of the grossest invasions of privacy on a massive and statewide scale.

Sometimes the County Councils were distressed by belligerent witnesses who simply refused to co-operate. A plaintive query from the Big Horn County Council to the State Council as to how to handle such witnesses brought this response from Secretary Greenfield:

> In two cases these men were brought before the County Council of Defense and while they persisted in their original decision, nevertheless public sentiment was so stirred up against them that they concluded it was part of wisdom to subscribe. In one case a genteel boycott was put on a man, in that he was not spoken to by any of his old friends, and in one instance he went into a store and the proprietor refused to allow him to be waited on. . . .

Secretary Greenfield went on to suggest that there were many ways of bringing a man to his knees. Another device was simply to take an ad in the local paper, saying "So-and-so is a slacker. Treat him accordingly."

The County Councils were also deeply involved in preventing speeches by non-patriots, such as members of the Non-Partisan League, which, second only to the I.W.W., stirred the ire of the patriots. The Non-Partisan League, an organization of dissident farmers, was not nearly as strong in Montana as in North Dakota, but it was strong enough to attract concerted opposition. Will Campbell's view was, as usual, a firm one.

> The Non-Partisan League, strikingly named the "Non-Patriotic League," aided by the I.W.W., the radical socialists and the pacifists, is laying the foundations for a Bolshevik movement which will overturn American principals [*sic*] of government and the strength already attained by this non-patriotic organization is so great and as yet so little realized by the people, that the situation is startling.

When one A. J. (Mickey) McGlynn, a Non-Partisan League organizer, appeared to speak before a group of farmers in Terry, the local council presented him with an oath that he would contribute $—— to the Red Cross; $—— to the Liberty Bond drive, and that if allowed to speak he would "not make any seditious utterances, or make any remark, the tendency of which would set up class hatred or community strife." He refused to sign. McGlynn moved on to Miles City without speaking in Terry.

There a mob, including "prominent businessmen and lawyers," took him to the basement of the Elks Club and beat him viciously. They then took him to the train and instructed him to leave town at once. This was too much for Sam Ford, the attorney general, who instructed the county attorney to bring charges against those involved. Ford himself went to Miles City, only to discover that whereas McGlynn himself had charged only five men, a smirking county attorney had arrested twenty-one, and a grinning justice of the peace discharged all of them at a preliminary hearing, without a word of evidence being introduced, this in Ford's presence.

Dozens of other cases of threats, beatings, and prohibitions of free speech had come to Ford's attention, and the McGlynn case prompted him to write a long letter to the Montana Council of Defense. The letter stands as a remarkable state paper, although it elicited no response from the council. Ford wrote:

> The right of free speech and the right to make public addresses have been denied individuals in the counties to which I refer by violence and in direct violation of the law, and the denial has been effected by intimidation and forcible coercion. Furthermore, it is common knowledge that in many cases, members of the county councils of defense have participated in these unlawful proceedings. The cases have been rather numerous. . . .
>
> It is true that we are at war and that the life of the nation is at stake; and these conditions may so affect the minds of over-zealous patriots and persons of hysterical tendencies as to lesson their powers clearly to analyze civil rights . . . but mob spirit is fraught with serious menace to society and to the most precious liberties of the people of the state. . . .
>
> I wish . . . to urge with all possible emphasis that the state council of defense . . . cooperate to the fullest extent of its powers . . . in the suppression of the lawlessness described and in the vindication of the right of free speech and the right to make public addresses in the state of Montana.

The council did not respond to Ford's letter; Will Campbell made no note of it in the *Independent*, no caution to the County Councils came forth. Nor did the council or the press note that three days later Congresswoman Jeannette Rankin was denied the right to speak in Deer Lodge "because of her I.W.W. and NPL leanings."

Many years later, U.S. Senator Burton K. Wheeler stood solidly opposed to Roosevelt's "court-packing" plan. Roosevelt sent Sidney Hillman of the C.I.O. to urge Wheeler to give up his opposition. Wheeler told Hillman that he had never forgotten his Montana experience during the First World War. He said, "Another hysteria might sweep this country and it might be against you people, or some other group, and when that time comes they will be looking to the Supreme Court to preserve their rights and uphold the Constitution." He refused to support Roosevelt.

The war ended, the super-patriots rolled up their flags, the Councils of Defense disbanded, and the beating of the drums ceased. In the quietness of the aftermath there must have been many second thoughts and somber reflections. At least B. K. Wheeler was elected to the United States Senate, Sam C. Ford was elected to the governorship, and Jeannette Rankin was returned to Congress.

The legislature sank back into its lethargy and never got around to repealing the Sedition Act—which appears on the statutes today, a strange anachronism.

VIII. THE UNIVERSITY
AND THE COMPANY

> It is entirely possible that the publication of Professor Levine's monograph may be the apparent occasion for slashing the University's appropriation, but the only cure for the present situation is the truth; surely we cannot endure indefinitely a state of affairs in which the publication of clear and scientific facts and principles can disrupt the state's highest institution of learning.
>
> President E. O. Sisson, University of Montana, 1919

THE vacuum left by the defeat of Germany and the consequent loss of a clear-visaged enemy in the form of spies, slackers, and saboteurs, was short-lived. Patriotism had been an enormously useful tool for those to whom dissent and change were frightful prospects. The great majority of Montanans had gone along willingly and often enthusiastically with the images created by the press in which the actions of labor and farm organizations, struggling essentially for better wages and working conditions, had been equated with disloyalty. The press had rarely drawn a line between the I.W.W. and the great bulk of laboring men. The Non-Partisan League and its predecessor, the Montana Society of Equity, had been tarred with the same brush.

The war ended. The Montana Council of Defense had issued its last order on October 7, 1918, in the form of a resolution addressed to President Wilson urging that the government not enter into negotiations with Germany, but "insist on the unconditional surrender" of the enemy. Most of

195

the County Councils dissolved themselves at the time of the Armistice. The State Council lingered on until 1921, occasionally worrying itself about the new threat—"Red Bolshevism."

It was the threat of bolshevism that filled the vacuum left by the war. If the pitch of emotion did not quite match the war years, it was there nonetheless—useful to some, frightening to others, food for innumerable editorials, and a continuing plague to labor and disgruntled farmers who could not escape the shadow of subversion.

Butte continued to simmer and occasionally to boil over, but federal troops were still there and they had become expert strikebreakers. The Company reduced its expenditure on detectives substantially. The press turned its attention from the I.W.W. to the Non-Partisan League.

By 1919, the honyockers' exodus from the state was well along. Farmers in general were suffering from depressed prices and dependence on the railroads, whose rates they considered too high. By 1920 the Non-Partisan League, which demanded basic economic and social reform for the farmer, had twenty thousand members in Montana—and they had Burton K. Wheeler as a champion. One of the issues, destined to arise again and again, was the gross lack of equity in taxation between the farmer and the miner, between agricultural and mining enterprises. It was this issue that engaged the attention of the University and brought the mailed fist of the Company forth once more.

Conflict could find no more incongruous setting than the garden-like and somnolent little town of Missoula. As lush and green as Butte was brown and barren, it had a population as homogeneous as Butte's was heterogeneous. True, it had a lumber industry, but its location at Bonner, seven miles to the east through a steep and curving canyon, removed the industry from the town. Butte had a population of 60,000 in 1920, Missoula of 8,000. Even at the height of I.W.W. activity, the citizenry had witnessed no violence, had seen no troops, and had never heard the clangor of riot. Nor were they destined to; the conflict was of a different nature.

In 1914, the Board of Education had passed a resolution which merely created as formal policy what was *de facto* policy in any event. The resolution read that the Board:

> . . . believes in the fullest and freest entertainment and expression of views relative to all public matters, on the part of the members of the faculties of the various state institutions. . . .
>
> Nevertheless, this Board is convinced that turmoil, agitation and intemperate discussion of public questions is inimical to the well-being, growth and success of the various educational institutions of this state.

Beneath the surface, however, there was ferment on the faculty. The inflexible parochialism of the pre-war years yielded a little as new faculty members replaced old ones. These new men came from the "outside," attracted, usually, by the pleasantness of the town and the magnificence of the surrounding country.

There were then four units of the University of Montana,[1] and the unwieldy structure had resulted in recrudescing turmoil. There had been an increasing demand for consolidation of the system, and gradually the president of the University at Missoula, E. B. Craighead, assumed the leadership of the

---

[1] The main liberal arts unit at Missoula, a School of Mines at Butte, a College of Agriculture and Mechanical Arts at Bozeman, and a Normal College at Dillon. There are today six units: University of Montana, Missoula; Montana State University at Bozeman; Western Montana College at Dillon; Eastern Montana College at Billings; Northern Montana College at Havre; and Montana School of Mines at Butte.

The University of Montana campus at Missoula, about 1920.
Courtesy University of Montana Library.

group demanding consolidation. Craighead was a blunt and articulate administrator, and he plunged with little hesitation into the fray. There was strong opposition to consolidation, however, not only from the areas in which the other units were located, but also from a group who believed that physical consolidation, as Craighead saw it, was not the answer. What the system needed, this group felt, was a chancellor, an "over-all-over-seer."

The battle soon involved the State Board of Education, the legislature and the governor, and on January 21, 1915, Craighead was summarily fired. He then founded a newspaper in Missoula, the *New Northwest*, which was destined to involve not only Craighead, but the University, in subsequent turmoil. Craighead was replaced as president by E. O. Sisson. The chancellor system was then adopted, and on February 1, 1916, Edward Charles Elliott was appointed chancellor of the University of Montana.

Elliott's credentials were first rate. He had a B.A. and an M.A. from the University of Nebraska; he had been superintendent of schools at Leadville, Colorado; and he had received his Ph.D. from Teachers College, Columbia University, in 1905, with a year of study sandwiched in at Jena, Germany.

Columbia Teachers College was then in the throes of experimental ferment, and Elliott's classmates were all subsequently to become prominent educators. From Columbia, Elliott went to the University of Wisconsin, was promoted to full professor in two years, and served as the university's director of teacher training. He wrote prolifically, and between 1905 and 1916, established close relationships with some of America's top educators, men like E. R. Seligman and A. O. Lovejoy. He was a fine public speaker; he had

Edwin Boone Craighead, President of the University of Montana, 1912–15. *Courtesy University of Montana Library*.

Edward C. Elliott, Chancellor of the Montana University System, 1916–22. *Courtesy University of Montana Library.*

202

demonstrable administrative ability, and, beyond peradventure, he had "connections."

He also had an administrative motto: "Watch your timing and be entirely neutral." The motto, as it turned out, was more of a key to what happened to Elliott, the University, and the state than all of the some hundreds of articles he wrote on education during the course of almost forty years in the field. He *did* watch his timing, which in critical periods was often abominable, and his "neutrality" was usually calmly ushered forth when almost anything but neutrality was called for.

Elliott himself emerged from his Montana experiences unscathed (at least outwardly), and he left to become the president of Purdue in 1922, where he remained until his retirement in 1945. But neither the University nor Montana was unscathed by the Elliott technique. Elliott, indeed, did not cause the problems; he sought persistently to avoid them. It was in the process of avoiding problems that he compounded them.

On February 7, 1919, Elliott suspended a professor, Louis Levine, for "insubordination and conduct prejudicial to the welfare of the University." The chancellor had informed neither the Board of Education nor the president of the University of his intention to fire Levine. President E. O. Sisson found the action "a painful surprise and sharp disappointment" as well as ". . . a heavy blow to the University and the state," and he wrote to Elliott, "I cannot express my grief at the apparent difference in our views."

The plight of Louis Levine might have gone unnoticed except for a series of circumstances that forced the issue into the open. Levine, an economist, was an "outsider," a new man. He had received his doctorate in sociology and economics at Columbia in 1912. He had served as an economic expert for the New York Department of Labor, had taught at Columbia and at Wellesley. He had studied not only in Russia, but in France and Switzerland. At thirty-six, Levine was an accomplished scholar, the author of several books and numerous articles, and he had not been long enough at the University to have come under the sway of the "old faculty." He did not, in any event, mix readily. He was cool and reserved, almost stiffly formal; a contemporary remembers him as being "almost European in his courtliness—a charming man, though always reserved."

In two and one-half years at the University, Levine had advanced from the rank of instructor to full professor. Both President Sisson and Chancellor Elliott endorsed this swift promotion enthusiastically. By the time of his suspension, he was widely admired by students and faculty alike. This admiration had a very positive bearing on the events that followed the suspension.

What actually led to the sudden and widespread interest in the suspension, however, lay in the investigations into tax inequities in Montana, which Levine had undertaken at the specific request of the chancellor. The irony of the situation did not escape Levine, but Elliott remained completely unaware of it. Elliott had indeed employed Levine to pry up the lid of a Pandora's box.

The tax structure as of 1919 was dear to the heart of the mining interests. They had planted that structure in the constitution itself as of 1889; they had fought to maintain it throughout the years. No threat to their interests was, in their estimation, more dangerous or fundamental.

Throughout the territorial period, mines had been almost tax free. The industry needed all the protection it could get, and from territorial legislatures composed largely of miners it got nearly complete tax exemption.

However, by 1889, the year of statehood, it was apparent that the industry, now glowing with health, ought to be taxed and ought to share the burden with agriculture and other business elements. The mines for the year 1887 had yielded over $25,000,000. By 1889, the annual output had risen to $40,000,000. Beginning in 1884, when an abortive constitutional convention was held, the agricultural elements had initiated a demand for the taxation of mines. By 1889 this demand had become so strong that, albeit reluctantly, the mining interests had come to the conclusion that some form of taxation was inevitable.

When the constitutional convention met in Helena in 1889, the miners came prepared with their own tax law, which they proposed to write into the organic act. The contention of the minority agricultural element—that specific provisions such as the nature of taxable assets and the method of taxing them were matters best left to the legislature—met the impassioned resistance of the miners. They proposed that mines should be "taxed at the price paid the United States," along with machinery, but that only *net proceeds* should be taxed.

W. A. Burleigh, an articulate representative from Miles City, the cow-country capital, pointed out that net proceeds could be easily manipulated and that, in effect, the miners were freezing into the constitution a tax exemption for the real wealth involved—the metal that came from the earth.

W. A. Clark was chairman of the convention. His answer to Burleigh was impassioned:

> If you study it as we have done, you arrive at no other

conclusion than that it is the only method whereby the state can secure from this species of property a reasonable and just revenue, and at the same time protect those men, those brave pioneers who have come out here and have made the wilderness blossom as the rose, and opened up these great mountains and brought their hidden wealth to light; yea, I say, it is the duty of the members of this convention to throw such safeguards around this industry as are proper and just.

The net-proceeds clause became part of the constitution of the state. This meant that mines were taxed "at the price paid the United States therefore," which was five dollars per acre for quartz mines and two and one-half dollars per acre for placer mines, a fixed valuation; that machinery could be taxed, but that only *net* proceeds could be taxed. In effect, net proceeds was defined as the gross product value less expenses; but expenses included everything having to do with operations. While county assessors were charged with the responsibility for determining these costs, obviously no assessor was equipped to do so.

The last territorial governor, P. H. Leslie, sounded the complaint, even before the constitution had been adopted, which was to be heard again and again throughout the years: "If you will take the pains to study the assessed values fixed upon the same class of property in different parts of this territory, there will be seen such glaring differences as to shock all sense of fairness and every principle of justice." Leslie went on to recommend the establishment of boards of equalization, to revise, harmonize, and equalize taxes.

Again in 1899, with Amalgamated now on the scene, Governor R. B. Smith assailed the legislature ". . . the only person who bears his full share and proportion of taxes is the farmer with a few acres of land or the citizen who owns a humble home in town or city. . . . The corporations . . . evade taxation on fully one-half of all they possess."

Smith's successor, Joseph K. Toole, told the legislature in 1903: "The burdens of taxation are most unequally distributed now. Millions of dollars of money and property escape taxation in this state year after year."

In 1912, Joseph M. Dixon, leader of the Progressive party, assailed Amalgamated: "These gentlemen are paying on the basis of about one-eighteenth of the real evaluation. . . . They should be paying about one-half the taxes of the state, on our present total assessment."

Dixon had spent two terms in Congress, had been elected to the U.S. Senate in 1907, had slipped over into the Progressive party and been defeated for the Senate in 1912. He ran on an anti-Amalgamated platform with the tax issue basic to his campaign. The party stationery carried the slogan, "Put the Amalgamated Out of Montana Politics." Dixon, though defeated, brought larger guns to bear on the tax problem than anyone thus far. Nor did his defeat alter the sentiment expressed in the party platform of 1912:

> We declare ourselves as being unalterably in favor of a complete reform of taxation laws and methods in Montana, to the end that there shall be a fair and equitable assessment of all classes of property. We believe that under present conditions railroads, the Amalgamated Copper Company, and other corporations are avoiding the payment of their just proportion of taxes. . . .

In 1916, the Republicans, now reunited with the Progressives, pledged themselves to a platform which called not only for reform of the tax structure, but threatened a constitutional amendment if legislation were not forthcoming. The Fifteenth Legislative Assembly, confronted with "an inadequate condition of state finances," a large deficit and the necessity of finding desperately needed new sources of revenue, appointed a Tax Investigation Committee. Company reaction was quick. The press sprang into action. "From remarks which have often been dropped in Helena this week," said the Anaconda *Standard*, "the natural inference is that mining companies are at present paying little, if any, taxes." The *Standard* went on to say that the Company was paying more than a fair share.

The Butte *Post* countered the legislative threat with the intimation that the agricultural interests of the state were "evading taxes." The Butte *Miner* said that, in truth, mining interests were bearing "an extraordinary tax not levied against any other industry in Montana." The *Miner* went on to say, "The miner has become so accustomed to paying his extra assessment that he no longer thinks of objecting to this discrimination against him." The paper labeled the group in the legislature urging tax reforms "agitators."

The Company machine slipped into operation on other levels. A speakers' bureau was quickly formed, and speakers briefed with figures and carrying colored charts fanned out over the state. Petitions began to pile up on the legislators' desks; "spontaneous" meetings of citizens were held.

In a petition to the legislature from the directors of the Butte Chamber of Commerce, the legislators were warned: "Commit an act which affects the business and prosperity of Butte's 90,000 souls and you immediately, in equal degree, affect the business and prosperity of some of Montana's largest and most important farming districts." The petition was signed by fifteen directors of the Butte Chamber, three of whom were officers of the Company. Company lobbyists were everywhere in Helena.

The Investigation Committee rendered its report. Its study revealed that gross proceeds for the year 1916 broke down as follows:

Mines	$141,500,000
Farming	81,154,190
Livestock	54,187,960
Railroads	60,199,998

The committee then paired the industries with the proportion of taxes paid, as follows:

Mines	8.79%
Farming	32.14%
Livestock	10.73%
Railroad	17.99%
Others	30.35%

The committee concluded:

> We believe that the large mining companies, the Hydro Electric Companies [Montana Power was closely allied with Anaconda] and the Pullman Car Companies are not paying their proportionate share of the State's taxes. We are also of the opinion that all these companies are abundantly able to respond to the needs of this state in the matter of revenue without injury to their business or in any manner jeopardizing the general welfare of the people of the state.

The report was not published by the Company press. The several tax reform bills were defeated handily; the legislature adjourned and the lobbyists went off for a week at Boulder Hot Springs to "dry out." The situation had never really been dangerous. Still, it would be well to keep an eye on things.

209

Dixon now owned a newspaper, the *Daily Missoulian*; he was still politically active; the Non-Partisan League was increasingly aggressive on tax matters; farmers generally were restive and angry.

The Company, in the name of the Montana Mining Association, prepared a pamphlet which it distributed widely throughout the state. It contained an analysis of the tax problem. It called the report of the Investigation Committee "illogical, impractical and impossible," "misleading and inaccurate," and "unfair and devoid of justice." It said that the theory that the industry should pay taxes according to gross income was "astounding" since, "a losing concern may do as much business gross as one making a large margin of profit." The rest of its presentation consisted of a slashing attack on the gross-tax proposal. The argument was impressively set forth.

If the farmers, the Progressives, and others were unhappy with the failure of the legislature to act, if they viewed the nearly thirty years of aggregate wealth that had come from the mines, compared it with the pittance represented by the net-proceeds tax and were distressed, Chancellor Elliott was equally disturbed. He was an ambitious man, and he saw no end to the fiscal shambles unless tax reform could be brought about. He saw no chance of increasing the woefully inadequate University appropriation unless such reform occurred. Louis Levine's teaching load was reduced and he was assigned the task of studying the entire tax structure with an eye to making recommendations for reform.

Levine's preliminary work led to several interim reports to the chancellor. Elliott was pleased. In December, 1916, he wrote Levine, "I have read . . . the reports . . . with an increased sense of my obligation to you for your interest and effort in this most important of our University problems."

Levine also contributed a series of articles, which appeared in January, 1917, in Joseph Dixon's *Missoulian*. Whether he was fully aware of Dixon's role *vis à vis* the mining interests is not clear, but Dixon called the articles a "splendid illustration of the service which the University can and should render the state," and he pointedly editorialized that Levine "has no axe to grind, no pet theory to defend, no special interest to support." Three months later, Levine contributed an article to the *Bulletin of the National Tax Association* entitled "Tax Legislation in Montana."

Now well into his general study of the tax structure, Levine was convinced that the nub consisted of mining exemptions. He proposed to Elliott that the first of a series of monographs concern itself with the root problem—mine taxation. Both Elliott and Sisson responded with enthusiasm. In the meantime, Elliott had "loaned" Levine to the State Tax Commission as a consultant.

In the spring of 1918, a Farmers' Tax Conference convened in Lewistown. The conference was part of the general agricultural unrest which was sweeping eastern and central Montana. It was the second year of drought, and while the state in general was as yet largely unaware of the rapidly accumulating agricultural problems, increasing numbers of farmers were joining the Non-Partisan League and talking of direct political action. While the railroads and non-resident grain companies headed the list of villains, tax reform stood high on the agenda of the angry farmers. Levine was asked to address this conference on mine taxation.

Chancellor Elliott promptly wrote to President Sisson recommending not only that Levine accept the invitation, but that his expenses be paid by the University because, he said, "It seems to be highly desirable that the University should make a contribution to the success of this enterprise."

The Farmers' Tax Conference attracted not just farmers. The Anaconda Company came to state its case—and it sent big guns. L. O. Evans, chief western counsel, and Dan Kelly, general counsel, both appeared and read lengthy papers. J. Bruce Kremer was also there, though he did not participate. In addition to his other widespread activities and his intimate Company connections, Kremer was a member of the Board of Education.

Levine spoke on mine taxation. He later wrote, "I had no manuscript and spoke without notes. I tried to state briefly and impartially the general problem of mining taxation." However impartial he may have been, Levine was not brief. His talk covers forty-three pages of transcript. He reviewed the entire problem in historical context and then presented statistics, using the Anaconda Company's own figures, and production and taxation figures from Arizona. He contended that mining interests in Montana were not paying a reasonable tax on net proceeds.

Evans, and then Kelly, answered Levine. Evans read a lengthy paper, and Kelly assailed "politicians and demagogues who attempt to stifle development." He referred to "poison peddlers" and "agitators" who "spread discontent and unrest." He called Levine "the gentleman from the University" and remarked, "If there is a high school boy in the state of Montana that could not give a better analysis of the situation that you gentlemen are trying to solve, I do not consider that he should have passed from the eighth grade."

Both Kelly and Evans in interchanges with Levine were sarcastic and abusive. Levine was persistent in returning to a statistical approach. Carl W. Riddick, congressman from the eastern district, who sat through the exchange, later spoke of Levine's performance as "impartial" and delivered "with the authority of a specialist," and he wrote Chancellor Elliott thanking him for Levine's participation and added that such frank and impartial presentations "tend to increase the public zeal and enthusiasm for the State University." J. Bruce Kremer of the Board of Education said nothing. Levine returned to Missoula to put the finishing touches on his monograph, now scheduled for publication by the University Press.

On June 20, 1918, at a regular meeting of the State Board of Education, J. Bruce Kremer demanded an investigation of two University professors who, according to Kremer, were "espousing socialism in their private teaching and public utterances." The professors were Levine and J. H. Underwood, chairman of the Department of Economics.

Elliott wrote Kremer two letters, one in June and one in July, endeavoring to ascertain what specific charges Kremer might have with respect to Levine. Kremer did not answer the letters.

In mid-November, 1918, Levine presented the first draft of his monograph to Elliott. It was forwarded with President Sisson's strong endorsement: "I do not know of anything which has been published in the Northwestern States which is equal to it. . . . This is the sort of work for which the University should have credit."

But the Board of Education met again in November with Elliott present. Ex-officio member Governor Sam V. Stewart queried Elliott as to why the Levine investigation had not been pursued. Elliott replied that Kremer had not laid before him "the documents from which the case seemed to originate." Stewart asked Kremer to report to the next board meeting.

213

Elliott was now disturbed. He wrote Levine that they should follow a policy of "watchful waiting" and added, "It may be fatal for us to force the issue at this particular moment." Elliott, belatedly, had looked behind the scene. The governor had been cool, if not hostile; Kremer had promised a full report; the rest of the board had been silent and uneasy. Clearly, there was danger.

When the board met again in December, Kremer presented excerpts from Levine's Lewistown speech. Obviously, these heretical ideas were socialistic; equally obviously, the University had no business involving itself in such affairs. Elliott was directed to reaffirm to the faculties of the University system that the policy of the board as stated in 1914 was firm, that "turmoil, agitation and intemperate discussion of public questions is inimical to the well-being, growth and success of the various educational institutions of this state."

Elliott now wrote Levine, "There is nothing to be apprehensive about. On the other hand there will be need of much circumspection during the next two or three months in order to avoid unnecessary and unwise complications." The problem was that there sat Levine's completed manuscript, strongly endorsed by Sisson, on the chancellor's desk. The further problem was that Levine, invariably courteous, but quietly determined, proposed to publish it elsewhere if the University did not do so, to which Elliott could hardly object.

The chancellor was given a brief reprieve when Levine departed for Washington at the request of Felix Frankfurter to do some urgent research for the War Labor Policies Board. When he returned in January, 1919, the chancellor immediately called him to Helena and informed him that under no circumstances could the monograph be published by the University Press. The governor, said Elliott, did not want the book published. When Levine agreed and said that he would seek another publisher, Elliott did not forbid him to do so, but warned him that "It would be better if I didn't, lest the 'interests' crush all liberal thought in Montana." According to Levine's view of the conversation, the agitated chancellor further warned him that he would be "brought up on trial on charges of socialism, Bolshevism, and so on" and that, "I would not get fair treatment in the press."

A week later the now obviously harassed chancellor wrote Levine, "Weighing all circumstances, it seems best for the larger and permanent interests of the University that *any* [italics mine] publication of this bulletin be indefinitely postponed." Although Levine was subsequently to insist that the chancellor never challenged his right to publish independently and never ordered him not to, a review of the chancellor's correspondence indicates clearly that this last communication was precisely such an order. Levine responded that he construed the prohibition, however, as applicable only to publication by the University and informed the chancellor on February 4, 1919, "I have decided to proceed with the publication of the bulletin. I sincerely believe that by so doing I shall best serve the general interests of the state and interests of the University."

The monograph entitled *Taxation of Mines in Montana* was published by B. W. Huebsch of New York City shortly after Levine's letter of February 4 had reached the chancellor. On February 7, 1919, the chancellor suspended Levine "for insubordination and conduct prejudicial to the welfare of the University." Clearly, if the chancellor had not been candid with Levine, neither had Levine with the chancellor. The publication date of the monograph indicates that Levine had decided at least several months previously (considering

215

press composition time for Huebsch) not to deal with the University Press. Clearly, too, he had informed neither Sisson nor Elliott of this decision.

Levine's suspension lifted the lid from the simmering anger of the agricultural elements; it struck fire from a university faculty suddenly no longer quietly subservient; it focused the critical lens of national publicity on Montana and the Company—and the glare, however momentarily, stripped the skin away from the hard and ugly sinews of control.

The Company press reacted predictably. The non-Company *Great Falls Tribune* followed suit. The University, said the *Tribune*, was "always a hotbed of scholastic intrigue and insubordination." The *Tribune* continued, "Professor Levine was born in Russia of Jewish parents . . . [he has] some reputation as a radical thinker and writer of economic subjects." Noting that the students were protesting Levine's dismissal, the *Tribune* remarked that "The socialists and radical elements in Missoula and other portions of the state had taken up the cry." And ". . . Much mischief comes from mixing politics with higher education. This Russian professor of economics had better take his views to Petrograd where they might be useful. . . . Controversial political questions are not healthy food for teachers of our young people to give out in the schools."

But the case had now attracted national attention. *The Nation* remarked editorially that although studiously moderate in tone, the book "was not a pleasant one for the mining companies to read." *The Nation*'s William MacDonald found the study ". . . a careful, thorough and scholarly piece of work" and added, "It is unnecessary to assume that the Anaconda Company or any of its agents asked for Professor

Levine's removal. . . . That would have been too crude a way of going about it."

The *New Republic* did not think so. Under the heading "The Professor and the Anaconda," the *New Republic* bluntly accused the Company of having engineered Levine's dismissal.

The case for tax reform was strongly buttressed by Levine's book itself. *The New York Times* remarked that the widespread publicity which attended the suspension "could not have been better conducted had Dr. Levine employed a staff of press agents." Thousands of Montanans who would otherwise never have read the book now did so. And although, as *The Nation* said, it was "somewhat severely technical" and "dispassionate," it was clear, even upon cursory reading, that Levine had written anything but a radical polemic. There was considerable perception in the *New Republic*'s view that "The Anaconda Company would be wise to insist on his reinstatement. Dr. Levine cannot possibly injure them so much by telling the truth about their tax-dodging as the university has injured them by trying to suppress it."

The Company press now faced a serious problem. To continue to vilify Levine, the students, and the University could only lead to a wider dissemination of the book. Abruptly, the press dropped the case.

Chancellor Elliott found himself in the rapidly closing jaws of a vise. The legislature, the very session he had hoped to approach for a much augmented budget, was in the process of considering a bill to abolish the chancellorship on the grounds that Elliott was "too socialistic for his position." Worse, a senate committee had been appointed to investigate

217

"socialism" at the University, and it proposed to question students and faculty. As Elliott was only too well aware, both students and faculty were thoroughly aroused.

Worse, as far as Elliott was concerned, was an impending investigation by the American Association of University Professors. Such investigations were thorough, could well lead to "blacklisting" the University, and were published in the widely read (in academic circles) *Bulletin of the American Association of University Professors*. The legislative investigation was scheduled for February, the AAUP investigation for March.

Other pressures were developing. Professor E.R.A. Seligman, the leading authority on taxation in the country, and Murray Haig, a prominent tax specialist, both of Columbia, added their voices to the growing praise for Levine's book.

Levine himself asked President Sisson to appoint a service committee to investigate the charges and report to the Board of Education. The committee consisted of Morton J. Elrod, professor of biology; Paul C. Phillips, professor of history; and Walter L. Pope, professor of law—three of the most distinguished professors on the faculty.

Thereafter, events moved rapidly. The Senate Investigating Committee made its report. It found no evidence to substantiate the charge that the faculty "taught socialism." The bill to remove Elliott was quickly killed.

The University service committee rendered its report on April 1, 1919—a scathing indictment of the Board of Education's policy forbidding faculty members from participating in public controversies. The committee asserted that the suspension had caused "irreparable harm" and "was calculated . . . to weaken the morale of the faculty and students, destroy

218

the confidence of the people of the state in the intellectual integrity of their educational institution, and to subvert all sound principles of educational policy. . . ." The committee further stated that Elliott's action had held the University of Montana up as ". . . a horrible example of narrow minded-ness, bigotry and intolerance." The committee sent the report to the Board of Education.

The investigation by the AAUP took place in March. The report strongly endorsed the stand of the service committee, deplored the action of the chancellor, criticized the Board of Education. Implicit in the report was a "blacklisting" of the University should Levine not be reinstated.

The pressure was too much for the Board of Education. It ordered the chancellor to reinstate Levine and to pay his back salary.[2] As if, somehow, to have the last word, it also passed a resolution endorsing the chancellor's suspension of Levine in the first place.

The reinstatement was widely regarded as a thumping victory for academic freedom by the faculty and others who had supported Levine. It was, however, a limited victory indeed. The real issue was never met because the real threat was never faced. The charges against Levine were never stated or released by the board. The chancellor never publicly explained his reasons for the suspension or the reinstatement.

2 Levine himself did not stay in Montana long. In 1921, he became a cor-respondent in Russia for the *Chicago Daily News*. He subsequently became a professor of economics at Beloit College, editor of *World Economics*, chair-man of the board of trustees of the National Economic and Social Planning Association, and a member of the research staff of the Brookings Institute. From 1935 to 1939, he was economic adviser to the International Labor Office of the League of Nations at Geneva. After World War II, he served as an economic adviser to the United States delegation to the General Assembly of the United Nations. See Arnon Gutfeld, "The Levine Affair: A Case Study in Academic Freedom," *Pacific Historical Review*, Vol. XXXIX (February, 1970), 19–37.

Everywhere the hand of the Anaconda Company left a nebulous mark, but nowhere its fingerprints.

The Levine case had clearly burned Elliott's fingers. But it apparently taught him very little except that the Company was an invincible antagonist. Even "watching his timing" and "being entirely neutral," he was soon in trouble again—or, more properly, the University was in trouble again, and Elliott's usual footwork moved him in the wrong direction.

On September 18, 1921, the Board of Education fired Arthur Fisher, an assistant professor of law. The board acted, it said, because of American Legion charges that called Fisher's patriotism into question and because he had engaged in "radical activities" in Missoula and because he was not a good teacher. The firing of Fisher stunned the University again. The "victory" in the Levine case was now suddenly washed down the drain.

Arthur Fisher was no Levine. In one short year on the faculty he had demonstrated a remarkable talent for alienating people. He was tactless, brilliant, and blunt, all of which was mingled with an almost ebullient physical energy. To Fisher, things were seldom gray. "The price of vigorous leadership," he said, "was usually opposition and often personal attacks." That did not matter. What did matter was the "social ameliorization and the betterment of the lot of the American laborer and his family, both in the city and on the farm."

Fisher, like Levine, was highly qualified. He was a graduate of Harvard Law School, where he had worked under Felix Frankfurter and Roscoe Pound. As was the case in Montana, Harvard could not absorb his almost boundless energies. He edited the prestigious *Harvard Daily Crimson* on the side; he worked with boys' clubs in the slums of Boston, and he served on the faculty of the Boston Trade Union College. When the war began, Fisher was working as a law clerk for a Chicago law firm. He was exempted from military service for a dislocated shoulder.

Fisher had participated in a "peace meeting" in Chicago in 1917, in which he had asserted that President Wilson should clearly set forth the war aims and the peace terms of the United States. He had signed, along with others, a statement that the meeting was "in no sense a protest against the present war . . . [but] the purpose of the war must be made clear to the people. . . ." Wilson's "Fourteen Points" had fully satisfied Fisher, who, in any event, was in no sense a pacifist.

When Fisher first arrived in Missoula, he went directly to the home of Martin K. Hutchens, the editor of the *Daily Missoulian*. Hutchens was also from Chicago and a mutual friend of Hutchens and Fisher had sent a letter introducing Fisher to Mrs. Hutchens. The friend had described Fisher to Mrs. Hutchens as "highly intelligent, well meaning, but radical and hasty," and had urged Mrs. Hutchens to advise Fisher ". . . to keep his mouth shut; to take no initiative; to praise but not to criticize for at least a year before attempting to reform Montana." If Mrs. Hutchens ever rendered the advice, Fisher ignored it.

Joseph M. Dixon had owned the *Missoulian* from 1913 to 1917. In 1920, the paper was owned by the Anaconda Company. As was often the case with Company papers, the details of this sale are obscure. Martin K. Hutchens was, as of 1920, listed as owner and editor of the paper. But he was not. Mrs. Hutchens, in a subsequent memoir, reported that her husband was "staggered" when he discovered that the Company owned the Seattle bank notes representing the principal stock in the paper.[3] Staggered or not, the *Missoulian* was a Company paper, and it was on the sharp point of this fact that the trouble revolved.

Within weeks after his arrival, Fisher was appearing at city council meetings and plunging headlong into community affairs. In spite of his initial friendly contacts with Martin Hutchens, he was soon loudly critical of the editorial policy of the *Missoulian*. He greatly admired Burton K. Wheeler, whom the *Missoulian* was busily excoriating. Also, he had met and was immediately attracted to E. B. Craighead and the editorial policy of the latter's *New Northwest*. Craighead and Hutchens were old enemies. Craighead and Fisher were new friends.

At the bitter height of the violent Wheeler-Dixon gubernatorial campaign of 1920, Craighead died. The *New Northwest* had never been entirely solvent, now it was in real financial trouble. Fisher stepped in to help raise money for the nearly moribund paper.

But his faculty duties, his interest in the *New Northwest*, his involvement in civic affairs, did not use up his energies. On the state level he began to agitate (in the Montana Teachers Association) for affiliation with the American Federation of Labor. The Montana Teachers Association had already attracted the ire of the Company for urging tax reform, especially in regard to mine taxation. Fisher now emerged as a radical, conducting an ". . . improper, un-American and dangerous" flirtation with the A. F. of L. The *Billings Gazette* pointed out that Fisher had been in Montana

---

3 See Sheila MacDonald Stearns, "The Arthur Fisher Case" (unpublished master's thesis, University of Montana, 1969), p. 10.

only three months, yet the responsibility for the corruption of the teachers' association was his and his alone.

At Thanksgiving dinner at the Hutchenses' house shortly after the teachers' convention, Fisher openly solicited the other guests of the Hutchenses for money with which to buy the *New Northwest* from E. B. Craighead's sons. That was the last time Hutchens and Fisher spoke, and from that time on, Hutchens declared open editorial warfare on Fisher and the *New Northwest*.

On December 8, the *Missoulian* first involved the University by stating that the University should keep "these tender footed goo-goos employed along certain definite lines and thus avoid further injury to the University from the mixture of the education of our youth with the stew of Montana politics."

Fisher began to retaliate with editorials in the *New Northwest*. The day after Hutchens' attack on him, Fisher replied with an attack on the Company. He deplored the fact that the press was "a subordinate adjunct of large scale business" and urged readers to keep the *New Northwest* alive to carry out "your ideals of a free press . . . subject to no other control whatsoever."

Within days, the Company press was in full cry. Will Campbell immediately demanded that the University "clean house." "It is learned," he wrote, "that two of the professors drawing salaries from the state of Montana, are engaged in organizing a socialistic newspaper . . ." and he was off, in his old form "radical," "I.W.W.," "poison," "red card socialism." Very soon the attack swung to include the whole University,

Overleaf: The University of Montana campus at Missoula in 1927. *Courtesy University of Montana Library.*

DORIAN STUDIO 1927.

which (by December 23), the *Independent* saw as "soaked in socialism." The question, said the *Independent*, "is whether or not we shall clean the University of Montana at Missoula of the socialist members of the faculty. . . . Given a little more rope and the professors who are behind the scheme to continue the publication of a radical newspaper in Missoula will demand that only those in harmony with the parlor bolsheviks be employed on the faculty. . . ."

The *New Northwest* countered quickly:

> An institution where faculty members are not entitled to the same rights and privileges as other citizens cannot by any stretch of the imagination be called a university.
>
> And when editors of such papers as the *Helena Independent* and the *Missoulian* are permitted, without formal protest from the people of the state, to lie about and attempt to browbeat prominent members of the faculty, it is disgraceful and humiliating, but it is nevertheless true, that we have not yet developed in Montana a real university.

At that precise moment, Chancellor Elliott may have understandably had a few chills. President Sisson had none. He was outraged—and he pressed Elliott to answer the charges in the *Independent* and *Missoulian* with the facts. Elliott refused ("watch your timing") and cautioned Sisson to remain silent. The other Company papers quickly took up the cry. Sisson wrote Elliott, "In no way has the University been at fault." These charges, he wrote, must be "nailed as false." And he bluntly told Elliott that there was no justification for "a permanent and continuous policy of silence on the part of the University. . . ." Elliott did not answer the letter; Sisson fired off another. He felt it "imperative," he said, to answer "the abuse and slander," and he informed Elliott that he intended, with counsel (including Dean C. W. Leaphart of the law school), to meet with Hutchens and to demand that the attacks cease. "As for the *Independent*," he wrote, "it will be remarkable if Fisher does not file suit for slander. . . ."

But Elliott had other plans ("stay neutral"). He was in touch with Hutchens himself. In fact, he had told Hutchens to quiet down, that he, Elliott, would handle Fisher. Hutchens wrote him, ". . . I had your assurances at our last meeting that the case of Mr. Fisher would be satisfactorily disposed of and that I need not worry about it. I am disposed to be patient in this matter and to await your action. . . ."

Fisher, like Levine, also wrote the chancellor setting forth his views in detail. The chancellor replied, proposing a personal conference at a later date. In spite of the fact that the chancellor visited Missoula several times, Fisher could not seem to pin him down for a conference. Hutchens, meanwhile, continued to write Elliott demanding action. Finally Elliott wrote Hutchens suggesting that he (Hutchens) should prefer charges against Fisher at the July meeting of the Board of Education. But the chancellor did not mail the letter.

Hutchens, in any event, took action on his own. He informed the officers of Missoula Post No. 27 of the American Legion, that they should investigate Fisher's activities at the "Terms of Peace" meeting in Chicago in 1917. The Legion post did so and the *Daily Missoulian*, four years later, grossly misquoting and distorting articles which appeared in the *Chicago Daily Tribune* on May 28, 1917, resumed the attack on Fisher with the announcement that the Missoula Legion post had demanded an investigation of Fisher on the basis of his loyalty to the country. The Legion post itself, however, conducted its own investigation and presented the next meeting of the Board of Education with its strong recommendation that Fisher be fired, ". . . that to subject the youth of this state to the influence of his teachings is to permit the undermining of the very foundation of our national safety."

It was July. Faculty and students were scattered. Fisher fought his case largely alone. Sisson, in utter disgust, had resigned the presidency in April and had gone off to teach at Reed College.

Fisher first answered the charges of the Legion in detail, both in writing and in person, and then answered them, in person, at the July meeting of the Board of Education. Furthermore, he took up the broader charges of radicalism and in a serious peroration said, "I believe thoroughly in an extension of the principles of democracy to industry and to the general economic sphere. . . . I believe that such an attitude is thoroughly conservative, in the best sense of the word. . . ." The July board meeting adjourned without acting on the Fisher case.

Between July and September, the press kept up a drumfire of criticism of Fisher and the University. The *Independent*, especially, was intemperate and almost always inaccurate, but the other papers, including the *Great Falls Tribune*, ran a close second. The *Tribune* remarked, "Professor Fisher . . . is said to be managing on the side a publication in Missoula which has been decidedly radical in its opinions upon public questions. The Board of Education should need only ten minutes to decide that this situation is not to be tolerated. . . ."

In none of the stories was it made clear that Fisher neither owned nor managed the *New Northwest*. He served as its legal adviser, he was on the newly reorganized board of directors, and he contributed an occasional editorial. But it was not his paper.

The new president of the University, C. H. Clapp, had come from the School of Mines. He quite simply did not like

228

Fisher. Fisher had, upon Clapp's accession to the presidency, written Clapp a letter, setting forth his views. The letter was lucid and dealt primarily with what Fisher believed his "case" to be all about, i.e., "academic freedom." In soft pencil, Clapp had scrawled across the bottom of Fisher's letter before filing it, "Troublemaker—not going to tolerate." He promptly informed Fisher that he was appointing a faculty "service committee" to review his (Fisher's) competence as a teacher.

The service committee, under the chairmanship of Professor Morton J. Elrod, conducted an exhaustive investigation of the American Legion charges, Fisher's teaching methods (they found him excellently qualified but not popular with his students), and his association with the *New Northwest*. They found the Legion's charges false and utterly without merit. They concluded that Fisher's *New Northwest* association violated no staff regulations or directives and did not constitute an activity with which the administration could legitimately interfere. The committee noted, in particular, that Fisher's "trouble" with the *Daily Missoulian* and the *Helena Independent* was probably due to his "aiding in the establishment of a rival newspaper." They concluded their lengthy report thus: ". . . we see no valid reason for terminating the contract of Mr. Fisher, as is evidently proposed." Clapp forwarded the report to Elliott.

At the September meeting of the Board of Education, Elliott "represented" Fisher. The latter was not present. He (Elliott) said that most "normal minded citizens" would support the Legion's charges. He said that Fisher's activities on the *New Northwest* had been detrimental to the University and that it violated the policy of ". . . maintaining a public university free from the destructive complication of class interests and partisan politics." As for teaching, said the

229

chancellor, Fisher had been ". . . content to render unsatisfactory and mediocre service to his students."

The Board of Education fired Arthur Fisher on September 12, 1921. The Company press chortled happily, and there was little reaction from the faculty or students. While the AAUP investigated the case, its report was not published until 1923, and its scathing indictment of the Board of Education went almost unnoticed.

Fisher was not Levine. He was abrasive, arrogant, and unpopular. Yet he was fired in violation of almost every tenet of academic freedom then extant. Martin J. Hutchens was no Will Campbell—and he had been personally affronted by Fisher. He was, moreover, a better than average journalist and a rational man. Yet he, along with Campbell and other Company press editors, twisted, distorted, and manipulated Fisher's public image, making a travesty of editorial integrity. The Company's role in the firing of Fisher is much more obscure than in the firing of Levine because of the role played by Hutchens. Yet there is little doubt that their press and its sustained campaign against Fisher was the key to his removal.

The University had been ravaged again. The report of the service committee, contrary to the rules of AAUP and the University's own regulations drawn up in 1915, had been ignored. The "Fisher Case" had other repercussions. E. O. Sisson, probably the ablest president the University had had, quit in disgust; Elliott, still watching his timing and being neutral, left in 1922 to become the president of Purdue; Martin J. Hutchens was fired in 1927, went to work for a new paper, the *Montana Free Press* in Butte, where he wrote vigorous anti-Company editorials.

Fisher went on to study in Europe, to write for *The Nation* and the *New Republic* and to practice law in Chicago. After

1940 he had a distinguished career in government service with the Library of Congress Copyright Division on the international agreements concerning copyrights, and he became the country's leading expert in copyright law.

The University of Montana and a hard core of faculty members who had twice challenged the "proper order of things" in Montana, sank into a lethargy from which it was not to recover for more than twenty years.

Even so, things were stirring in Montana in 1921. Progressivism had been held at bay for a long time while it swirled around the perimeter. But Burton K. Wheeler was still stumping the state, Joseph M. Dixon was the newly elected governor—and neither the removal of Levine or Fisher had quieted an increasingly vocal number of angry and reform-minded Montanans.

IX. THE PROGRESSIVES
MAKE THEIR MOVE

> 1920 was *l'année terrible* for the Company and
> its supporting interests. . . . In view of the previous
> bitter antagonism between A.C.M. and these two
> men (Wheeler and Dixon) the former could not
> even find the usual solace in that natural corporate
> hope that they were merely talking for the voters.
>
> Jules Alexander Karlin, "Progressive Politics in
> Montana," *A History of Montana*, by Burlingame
> and Toole.

T HAT Joseph M. Dixon and Burton K. Wheeler were
both candidates for the governorship of Montana in the fall
of 1920 was testimony not merely to unsettled times, but to
the fact that there were limits to the Company's control of
events and hence of men. It was, indeed, a bad time for the
Company—and it was a bad time for Montana. The great
drought burned relentlessly in the east. In the west, labor in
the mines and the wood camps was still sullen and restive.

Neither Dixon nor Wheeler had come forth as dark horses
to meet the exigencies of the myriad problems which had
surfaced in the last few years. Both men had already been
tempered in the crucible and were well known to Montanans.
Dixon had been Montana's lone congressman in 1903. He
had moved up to the Senate in 1907. He had served intelli-
gently but without particular distinction until about 1910
when, in the view of regular Republicans, he began to go
astray. He first startled the regulars by espousing a federal
income tax and then quickly alienated the powerful railway

lobby by vehement support of a "long and short haul" amendment to railroad legislation then being considered by the Senate.

Back in Montana he began to talk about a direct primary, and, worse, about tax reform on the state level. In the legislative session of 1911, pro-Company–anti-Dixon elements surfaced openly, and Dixon responded with renewed vigor in support of the direct primary. He said, "I am indeed sorry that the recent session of the Montana legislature did not enact a primary election law, and am not unaware of the real sources of opposition to the measure. . . . The great handicap . . . is the ease with which the great corporate interests can control conventions and legislatures." Dixon spent more and more time in Montana stumping for the primary law, for fiscal reform, and by the fall of 1911, he was openly accusing Anaconda and the railroad interests of chloroforming "enough senators and members" to prevent electoral reform.

By 1912, Dixon had broken completely with the Republican party, which he considered to be wholly controlled by the Company, and had become a Progressive. Moreover, he took over the management of Theodore Roosevelt's pre-convention campaign which dispersed his efforts and too often left the stage to his enemies at home.

This might have pleased the Company except that behind each threat stood another. A young, coldly blue-eyed, anti-Company Democrat, Thomas J. Walsh, a liberal Helena attorney, was also interested in the Senate. He had served in the legislature with B. K. Wheeler, had been once defeated for the Senate, but he was still widely liked and admired. He and Wheeler were close friends, and Walsh was indebted to Wheeler for the latter's unwavering support, in the face of violent Company opposition, in Walsh's unsuccessful bid for the Senate. The Company not only had to deal with Dixon, but now with Walsh and, worst of all, with the implacable Wheeler. They made the only real choice open to them, and Walsh was elected to the Senate in 1912.

Dixon, however, was far from discouraged. He and Roosevelt had run well in Montana. They had far outdrawn the Republicans and had run only a few thousand votes behind the Democrats. Dixon bought a controlling interest in the *Daily Missoulian* (not then a Company paper) and sat back to await developments.

Walsh arranged for the appointment of B. K. Wheeler as United States District Attorney, from which office Wheeler tilted and jousted with the Company, the Montana Council of Defense, and the conservatives in his own party, while solidifying his support in the Non-Partisan League and in other "radical" circles.

Wherever the Company looked in the years between 1918 and 1920 there were dark and ominous clouds on the political horizon. There was Wheeler and there was Dixon. There was also a spellbinding young Republican, Wellington D. Rankin, and his sister, Jeannette, who, with strong Non-Partisan League support, had become the first woman elected to Congress in 1916. And there was Sam C. Ford, restive as a Republican attorney general, angry with red-baiting politicians and at odds with the Company.

There is evidence that the Company, which had long (and with icy pragmatism) worked within any and all parties or political groups, now found itself in strange and somehow hostile waters. Its press, particularly during the campaigns of 1918 and 1920, often seemed rattled. In part, at least, this was due to a new element in an old picture. Farmers had joined labor in a political bid for a redress of grievances. It was not a formal alliance; the common glue was anger and frustration on a wide basis, ranging from railroad rates and high prices to corporate control of the machinery of government. The Company's influence on labor, including the control of bloc votes, was an old story. But the farmers were something else. The Company could hardly work through the Non-Partisan League. It held no axe over the farmers' heads. A threatened shutdown of smelters and mines, the old Company ploy when labor became particularly restive, meant nothing to the farmer—especially when his wheat was already shriveling in the hot fields and the banker was threatening to call his note.

If the Company's position was difficult, T. J. Walsh's was worse. When Walsh had engineered Wheeler's appointment as U.S. District Attorney he had given the latter some sound, if somewhat avuncular, advice. He was still deeply grateful to Wheeler for his rocklike support in his (Walsh's) first bid for the Senate. He was aware of what courage this took for a legislator from Butte. He had paid that debt, in part at least, with Wheeler's appointment to the district attorneyship. But Wheeler still worried Walsh. Soon after the appointment he wrote Wheeler, "We are looking to see you make a record in the office and there are opportunities in connection with it of which I am sure you are fully appreciative." But he admonished Wheeler to be "cautious and not allow the strenuous political contests through which we have passed to bias your judgment."

But neither then nor later was Wheeler the politician Walsh

Congresswoman Jeannette Rankin and her brother Wellington D. Rankin. *Courtesy Montana Historical Society.*

was. He could not resist contest; he could not paper-over his bitter animosity to the Company. He was unalterably aggressive—and his rough tactics in Montana soon began to embarrass Walsh politically.

Early in 1918, Wheeler made a speech at the annual convention of the Montana Society of Equity, in which he heartily welcomed the Non-Partisan League into Montana. He railed at corporate control of Montana's political structure from then on. He was quickly embroiled with the Montana Council of Defense over sedition and espionage. Within months of his appointment he had alienated not only the entire "establishment," but also the most ardent supporters of Walsh who had come to regard him as Walsh's greatest political liability.

Walsh repeatedly expressed his concern to Wheeler and pointed out that his reappointment as U.S. District Attorney was contingent, in effect, on his (Walsh's) own success. Wheeler's reaction was typically blunt. "If I am reappointed," he wrote, "you will lose some friends. If I am not reappointed you will lose a great many. . . ."

This pointed up a dilemma of which Walsh was completely aware. He did not have sufficient support within the regular structure of his own party to win re-election. He had to put together an unlikely coalition to win. He needed, first of all, at least the neutrality of the Company. He needed, also, considerable support from the disgruntled farmers and laborers. That meant that he could not afford to alienate the Non-Partisan League—and they were strongly in favor of Wheeler's reappointment.

Moreover, after losing in the Republican primary, Jeannette Rankin had filed as an Independent and she, like Wheeler, had strong labor and farm support.

Thomas J. Walsh, United States Senator, 1918–24. *Courtesy Montana Historical Society.*

After an agonizing early spring, Walsh recommended the reappointment of Wheeler on April 8, 1918. He saw no other course to take, balancing all factors. But he was unprepared for the ensuing uproar. By mid-summer, even Wheeler began to appreciate the extent to which he was "a lodestone" around Walsh's neck and he offered to "sacrifice all my pride and send in my resignation to the Attorney General." At first an anguished Walsh refused, but as the hot summer wore on into an equally hot fall, as Jeannette Rankin's campaign gained momentum, as the Company press continued its vitriolic campaign against Wheeler (but maintained a curious silence about Walsh), Walsh changed his mind and withdrew his nomination of Wheeler. He was re-elected in November by a plurality of less than 6,000 votes.

Walsh's law partner in Helena, C. B. Nolan, wrote him on November 7: "The election returns show most conclusively that the Company did all that it possibly could to bring about your election, and without the financial assistance that was given by Con Kelley, our situation would be critical. . . ."

Walsh's principal biographer[1] insists that Walsh made no "deal" involving Wheeler, and that he "did not become a corporate tool when he yielded on Wheeler and secured Company backing in this election . . . during the campaign Walsh was under terrific pressure and faced political realities, among which was defeat if he did not win Company support."

Walsh, of course, went on to become a distinguished senator, particularly subsequent to his breaking of the Teapot Dome case in 1924. He had been appointed attorney general of the United States by Franklin Roosevelt just prior to his death in 1933. There is no doubt that he faced political

---

[1] J. Leonard Bates, "Senator Walsh of Montana, 1918–1924: A Liberal Under Pressure," (Ph.D. dissertation, University of North Carolina, 1952).

realities in 1918, and there is no doubt that he continued to face them during the rest of his career. But "deal" is a word with various shades of meaning. From the standpoint of the Progressives remaining on the local scene (particularly Wheeler and Dixon) a "deal" most certainly had been made. Though Dixon had never been personally close to either Wheeler or Walsh, he is presumed to have said after Walsh's election (though the story is probably apocryphal), "Well, we were three and now we are two."

As for Wheeler, he made no secret of his disgruntlement. Not only did he refuse to campaign for Walsh, but he left no doubt in anyone's mind but that in his view the road to political success in Montana (a road across which the Company stood inevitably athwart) followed the trails of the earlier Progressives. The only honorable tactic was the hot pursuit of those goals.

By 1920 things had grown worse in Montana. The drought was burning into its third year; wheat prices had plummeted; more than a hundred banks had failed, and others were on the near edge of failure; county indebtedness had multiplied frighteningly, and all that an impotent special session of the legislature in 1919 could suggest was that the stricken agricultural counties sell bonds and put indigent farmers to work on county roads. But there was no one to buy the bonds. The Non-Partisan League had twenty thousand members and was rapidly becoming a powerful political force in the state.

There were other problems. The "red scare" that afflicted the entire nation was virulently abroad in Montana. Labor was more than restive; it was explosively dissatisfied and the Montana Labor League joined the Non-Partisan League in the cry for reform. The drought, strikes, and the exodus of farmers from taxable land had plunged the state into a deepening deficit. Louis Levine's figures on mining taxation were quoted at farm and labor meetings all over the state.

In this shifting milieu, Dixon and Wheeler both sought the governorship—Wheeler forging a coalition of farmers, laborers and "radicals" in the Democratic party, Dixon appealing to the "moderate" element, strongly anti-Non-Partisan League, led by the Republican party. The State Supreme Court had recently upheld the constitutionality of Montana's direct primary act, and the Company ran "vote-splitting" candidates in both Democratic and Republican primaries. But Dixon and Wheeler both won handily—they were simply too well known to be beaten by the quickly dredged up faceless men with whom the Company sought to defeat them. Walsh campaigned actively for Wheeler and Theodore Roosevelt bombastically endorsed Dixon. The Company was left with a choice almost too bitter to contemplate.

On the sixth floor of the Company's Hennessey Building in Butte, L. O. Evans, Con Kelley, J. Bruce Kremer, and Dan Kelly held a disconsolate war council a few days after the primary. Dixon or Wheeler, Wheeler or Dixon? Wheeler had been their nemesis for a full decade. He represented everything they detested and feared. Dixon was manifestly dangerous because of his views on mine taxation, in particular, and his progressivism in general. But, in fact, it was not a matter of flipping a coin. One factor was overriding. Another hot summer was sliding into another hot fall, and from the vantage point of that year of 1920 the most frightening thing imaginable was the prospect of a coalescing alliance of the Non-Partisan League and resurgent labor under the aegis of a Democratic party led by "Bolshevik" Burton K. Wheeler. The Company would back Dixon—or, rather, and the distinction was less fine than it seems in retrospect, it would defeat Wheeler. Then, once in office, Dixon would be dealt with.

One of the tributes to the fact that the times were indeed out of joint lies in the fact that the Company press, usually so well oiled that it could change political direction with nary a squeak between a morning and an afternoon edition, found itself flustered. The Butte *Miner*, even as late as September 13, could only complain:

> Usually it is possible to choose the lesser of two evils. As far as the *Miner* has investigated the situation, it is unable to satisfy itself up to date, that there is any lesser evil offered in this particular case.

Will Campbell's Helena *Independent* got around a direct endorsement of Dixon simply by reporting what Montana's senior senator, Henry L. Myers, had to say in his favor. But as the campaign progressed, the *Miner*, *Independent*, Anaconda *Standard*, and the other papers swung into line, although they continued to stress that this was more of a campaign *against* socialism, bolshevism, and anarchy than a campaign *for* Dixon. The small western town of Hamilton's invincibly independent *Western News*, edited and owned by the brilliant and puckish Miles Romney, enjoyed the discomfiture of the Company press enormously. The campaign, he said, was between Mr. Dixon, "who evidently was a 'Bolshevist' and flirted with the Non-Partisan League up to the moment they nominated another" and Mr. Wheeler, "a Jeffersonian Democrat, who is now denounced as a 'Bolshevist.' " And Romney added, "Since both Mr. Dixon and Mr. Wheeler are, or have been, 'Bolshevists,' what are the good people who are 'seeing red' going to do about it?"

Wheeler's campaign was frenetic—and it attracted ex-

243

tremists and dangerous hostility. For some years after the election of 1920 he was known in unfriendly circles as "Boxcar Burt," the appellation dating to a campaign speech in Dillon, where he narrowly missed being tarred and feathered and escaped only at the last moment on a freight train. When he was denied a hall in Miles City, he spoke from a hayrack on the edge of town. He excoriated the Company at every opportunity. He urged upon farmers and laborers a permanent political alliance as the only answer to the ills of the state and the only effective means of putting the Company out of politics, out of the newspaper business and back into the mining business, where it belonged.

The press, of course, was almost universally hostile and, in posters which were plastered all over the state, Wheeler was accused not only of being a bolshevist, a revolutionist— and either a drunk or a dry, he was even pictured as an advocate of "free love."

Dixon's campaign was very carefully plotted and skillfully conducted. He was aware that his "defection" of 1912 had not been forgiven by many Republicans. He was equally aware, however, that his Progressive record would do him no harm in farm and labor circles. He knew that Wheeler would carry the "hard core" radicals and he (Dixon) expected no support from the Non-Partisan League or the Montana Labor League. The tenor of his campaign was set by his own press release announcing his candidacy for the primary. He talked about extremism and its dangers. Neither the Non-Partisan League nor "the reactionary industrial interests," he said, were interested in the welfare of the majority of Montanans. He believed that the average voter wanted a sane and intelligent approach to pressing social and economic problems. In effect, he repudiated both the league and the

Joseph M. Dixon, Governor of Montana, 1921–24. *Courtesy University of Montana Library.*

245

Company as representing the extremes and proposed to go down the middle.

This rendered him vulnerable, of course, to attacks from both left and right, and it was in this regard that the press assumed critical importance. Dixon was not worried about the primary because he correctly foresaw that the Company would enter numerous vote-splitting nonentities. Only Sam C. Ford concerned him, but he did not believe that the attorney general had the power of the press. But how would the press react to Dixon? The question plagued him. Early in the primary, however, with a few exceptions, the pattern began to emerge.

The papers did not give his carefully prepared speeches detailed coverage. They abstracted his anti-Non-Partisan League, anti-socialistic statements and let it go at that. They frequently buried their stories in the inner pages. The Billings *Gazette*, for instance, responded to a thoughtful hour-and-a-half address at a Billings rally three days before the election with a two-inch story on page two. This kind of treatment, which under ordinary circumstances would spell trouble for any Montana politician, satisfied Dixon completely. Wheeler had the front pages, and Dixon was happy that he did. Other Company candidates in local areas received solid press support, which did not trouble Dixon.

A few papers, such as the Helena *Record-Herald,* gave Dixon's campaign genuine coverage. It is from such scattered sources that one gets a glimpse of the real candidate behind the clichés. If the Company was listening (and when were they not?), occasionally a chill wind must have swept the corridors of the Company's Hennessey Building—because shining between the *pro forma* excoriations of "radicalism" were thoughtful and informed comments about the dangerous state deficit, the need for a more equitable tax system, the need for a constitutional convention, a reform of state and local government structures, practical recommendations for economic aid to hard-pressed farmers, and a generalized progressive format which almost *in toto* would be anathema to the Company if seriously undertaken by any governor.

Dixon and Wheeler won the primaries handily. The general election campaign started at once. The pattern of the primaries was now repeated, except that, with only the two candidates in the field, Dixon's press coverage greatly improved. It was now, said the *Missoulian*, "Dixon or the Deluge"; what flag, the editor asked, did Montanans want flying over the capitol, ". . . the red flag or the American?" The Butte *Miner* said that the issue was now ". . . sane government versus half-baked socialism." The Anaconda *Standard* under a headline, "Montana at Parting of the Ways," said that it was simply a matter of freedom versus Socialist slavery.

Only a few remote and independent weeklies, such as the *Dawson County Review*, also played up the fact that Dixon balanced his anti-Non-Partisan League remarks with sentiments strongly expressed that tax reform was a vital necessity and that he wanted to see state government moved from the Hennessey Building in Butte to Helena.

On several occasions, Will Campbell, of the Helena *Independent*, simply could not sustain his pro-Dixon façade. A rumor arose to the effect that early in the campaign Dixon had sought Non-Partisan League support. Dixon vigorously denied it. In an initial editorial, Campbell said that he preferred to accept Dixon's word. Three days later, Campbell changed his mind and boldly stated that he simply did not believe Dixon's story.

247

The Butte *Miner* also had trouble, refused to deny the validity of the rumor, and said that it would withhold judgment until further information was provided. Both the *Independent* and the *Miner* had other lapses and throughout the campaign their "support" was generally unenthusiastic. The switch from virulent anti-Dixonism to pro-Dixonism was simply too much for the Company. For Will Campbell, particularly, it was a bitter pill, and the taking of it was assuaged only by the fact that he could malign Wheeler to his dark mind's full capacities.

Dixon defeated Wheeler by an overwhelming 37,000 votes. Indeed, Dixon had polled more votes than Warren G. Harding. It was a complex election turning on complex local issues, but at root, Dixon's triumph and Wheeler's defeat were readily explainable. Montanans were not yet distressed enough to react favorably to a Democratic party in the guise of a radical Non-Partisan League—especially in a year of Republican ascendancy in the country as a whole. Democrats and Independents flocked into Republican arms. The election marked the end of the Non-Partisan League's influence in Montana. And, ironically, it marked the beginning of the end for Joseph M. Dixon and the end of the beginning for Burton K. Wheeler.

Once more the war counsel assembled in Butte. But the picture was clear now. Very clear. Wheeler was out, more resoundingly defeated than any gubernatorial candidate in the state's history—a defeat from which his enemies believed he could never recover. Walsh was safely tucked away in Washington, an outspoken liberal on the national scene, a cautious, middle-of-the-road politician at home, at essential peace with all contending factions. So that left Joseph M. Dixon.

The gears shifted, the guns turned smoothly. The administration of Joseph M. Dixon began.

X. THE END OF
PROGRESSIVISM 1920-24

> Anaconda, a company aptly named, certainly has a constrictorlike grip on much that goes on, and Montana is the nearest thing to a "colony" of any American state. . . .
>
> John Gunther, *Inside U.S.A.*

IN late December, 1920, the outgoing governor, S. V. Stewart, packed his personal files and mementos and left the red plushness of the governor's office with a sense of almost euphoric relief. It had not been *all* bad for him. For a while, during the war, he had even had a sense of high mission. He had, he felt, been successful in stimulating agricultural production, in stopping subversion, in working closely with the Company in the greatly increased mineral production so necessary to the war effort. In fact, his first term had really been a very good one for him and, he felt, for the state. In 1912 he had won by only a little over 3,000 votes; in 1916, he had won by over 9,000 votes. Obviously, Montanans had approved of his policies. The trouble had come later. The last three years of his second term were something of a nightmare. Things seemed, somehow, to fall apart.

Except for the drought, which was, after all, an act of God about which a politician could do very little, the disintegration of things struck him as pointless. What real complaint did these troublemakers have, after all? What business did a *university* have fooling around with the tax structure? Wheeler, Dixon, and "that ilk" he failed utterly to understand. But the bitterness and outrage of the farmers and workers troubled him deeply. He was inclined to agree with Con Kelley that they had simply been gotten to by "poison peddlers" and "agitators."

He was deeply troubled, too, because in spite of the obvious acumen of his advisers, men like Kelley, L. O. Evans, and Kremer, state finances were in a shambles. The trouble was that he did not really know how they had gotten that way. Men like Dixon kept throwing figures around—a farm mortgage debt of almost $200,000,000; Montana farm income and wages were down, but living costs across the U.S. had risen 88 per cent since 1913; the state itself was confronted with a $2,000,000 deficit. There was widespread demand for tax reform, but what kind of reform? Stewart found any tampering with the constitution abhorrent, and he certainly did not think that the mining industry, which the state so desperately needed, should bear a heavier burden than it already bore.

He could and did write Dixon off as a demagogue. But what of the others? His files were bulging with letters of complaint and demands for action from responsible people—including both the senior and junior senators from Montana.

C. B. Nolan, Walsh's law partner, had reported to Walsh that Montana was in "woeful condition. There is no industry that is carried on that is not in a state of collapse. The sheepmen, the cattlemen and the farmers are practically broke." Such complaints were forwarded to Stewart who sought to blame things, usually plaintively, solely on the drought. Indeed, the drought *was* devastating, but as Stewart well knew, everything else was also awry. The special session of the legislature in 1919 was as unable as Stewart to come to grips with real problems. Now Stewart was leaving office and Joseph M. Dixon was taking over.

If the times did not auger well for Dixon, politics seemed to. The Republicans had made a clean sweep. Wellington D. Rankin was attorney general; the lieutenant governor was Nelson Story, Jr.—the other elected positions in the executive branch were all filled by Republicans. In the senate the Republicans outnumbered the Democrats forty to fourteen. In the house, it was ninety-eight to ten.

Under normal circumstances, this would have meant a mandate and the Company press lost no time in pointing out that it was a mandate *against* radical action and irresponsible experimentation. Will Campbell, pointing to the deficit, quickly reminded Dixon that no tax proposals should be put forth "injuring or confiscating any man's business or property," (i.e., a change in mine taxation would be unwelcome).

Although strong Republican control of both the legislative and executive departments seemed to give Dixon a powerful base for aggressive action aimed at fundamental problems, this was, as Dixon well knew, largely illusory. As Rae Logan, a close friend and confidante, remarked, "After all, this was the *Montana* legislature, not just a legislature. It was a kept body, not an independent assembly."

Dixon was also aware of the fact that the Republicans had by no means recovered from the split of 1912, that old enmities and resentments were very much alive, and that if the Democrats had been torn asunder in 1920, the Republican structure was like a block of ice frozen to brittle fragility. Republican solidarity could not, in other words, survive even a small, sharp blow.

In December, 1920, a special dispatch from Marion, Ohio,

stated that Dixon was being considered by President-elect Harding for secretary of the interior. He was not, but that is beside the point. The reaction of the Company press was revealing. The Lewiston *Enterprise* was enthusiastic. "We are convinced that Mr. Dixon will serve Montana better while serving the West and the nation as Secretary of the Interior than he can as governor." Will Campbell had a moment of near ecstacy—and strongly urged Dixon to accept. The *Missoulian* spoke of his "incomparable fitness for the place." Miles Romney of Hamilton's *Western News* was amused: "Would Anaconda," he asked, "rest easier if Mr. Dixon were in Washington than in Helena?" The answer, of course, was that it would, indeed. But on December 30, Dixon announced that he had no interest in the secretaryship at all, and the momentary hope of the Company came to naught.

Dixon is a difficult man for historians to come to grips with. The motivations of Walsh and Wheeler emerge with some clarity. Dixon's remain obscure.[1] Yet one cannot read

[1] Wheeler's own memoirs, *Yankee from the West* (with Paul Healy), Doubleday, 1962, is revealing and fascinating reading. Richard Ruetten, "Burton K. Wheeler of Montana: A Progressive Between Wars," Ph.D. dissertation, University of Oregon, 1961; Joseph Kinsey Howard, "The Decline and Fall of Burton K. Wheeler," *Harper's Magazine*, March, 1947, and other theses and articles are all helpful in understanding Wheeler, although Wheeler's papers, *per se*, have been available to no one but Healy and are not accessible to researchers. Mr. Wheeler has been very liberal and gracious in granting interviews to and answering letters from sundry scholars.

The Walsh papers are in the Library of Congress and have long been available, and J. Leonard Bates, "Senator Walsh of Montana, 1918–1924," Ph.D. dissertation, University of North Carolina, 1952, as well as Bates's excellent study, *The Origins of the Teapot Dome*, the University of Illinois Press, 1963 (and other articles by Bates), give great insight into Walsh.

Dixon's papers are in the Archives of the University of Montana and are restricted until the forthcoming biography by Jules Karlin of the University of Montana is published. Karlin's study should rectify the eclipse which has long characterized the career of Dixon.

Dixon's State of the State message of January 4, 1921, to the Seventeenth Legislative Assembly of Montana without admiration and even amazement. It is striking, first of all, because it sets forth a program which, if adopted in 1970, would render state government in Montana infinitely better than it is. It is remarkable for the insight Dixon brought to bear on fundamental economic, political, and social ills which plagued Montana in 1920 but which (more compellingly, still) afflict the state in some degree even today. It is a document of penetrating clarity in which there is almost no partisanship. It is marked by utter candor. Yet, without supporting charts and graphs, it is only twenty-eight pages in length.

Whatever Joseph M. Dixon's ambitions may have been and whatever complexities may have marked his motivations up to the time of his election to the governorship in 1920, there is no doubt that Montana now had a governor who saw with amazing clarity what was wrong and how it could be rectified.

He pointed out that Montana had just passed through four of the most trying years of her history. He asserted that during the war her young men were drafted upon a population basis of 940,000 while the true population had been only 548,889 (a mistake which has never been explained to this day). The consequence, he said, was that Montana sent 40,000 young men to war, nearly double the quota of any other state. He observed that Montana's war bond quota (which had been met and exceeded) was based on the same miscalculation. The young men were not returning in the proportion they should because "our interior geographical location prevented us from sharing in the financial prosperity that came to communities more favorably situated." And he said, "With the forward looking, optimistic spirit of the West, we have gone

forward, sometimes, I fear, not heeding or counting the ult
mate financial cost."

He referred to the drought and the actual severity of th
economic consequences. And then he plunged into the hea
of the matter. The situation, he said, "compels me to candidl
call your attention to the financial situation that now cor
fronts us in state and county and municipal governments.

The general fund, he said, was overdrawn $2,129,447
outstanding deficiency claims would increase this to $2,529
447. But, he pointed out, ". . . this does not tell the real story,
for if that deficit were projected with no new taxes and n
new revenue due to natural growth in mind, "I know of n
legerdemain of finance that will permit state government t
function during the coming year, under the present system c
taxation, revenues and expenditures." He added, "But th
embarrassment that confronts the people of Montana is by n
means confined to state government itself." State debt, h
said, is a mere bagatelle "when compared with the cost c
local governments in the counties, municipalities and schoc
districts."

He followed these opening statements with detailed stati
tics and concluded, "The truth is that taxes on real estate hav
reached the point where it now threatens confiscation. . .
We might as well face this fact: Intangible and invisibl
wealth is not bearing its proportion of the burden of taxa
tion." Meaning what? Meaning first of all, that, as mo
states had long since done, we must establish an income ta
an inheritance tax, a license tax on public service corpora
tions and *the great industrials* [italics mine]. Our tax systen
he said, was archaic, unscientific, and not adjusted to moder
economic conditions.

Startling enough for Montana in the year 1920, but ther

was more. He advocated a three-per-cent gross tax on oil. Montana dry farming sections, he said, "are now literally staggering, at a time of severe depression . . . under heavy taxation." Yet Montana coal mines in the year 1919, mines owned largely by the Northern Pacific Railroad, produced in excess of 3,000,000 tons of coal. They showed little taxable "net proceeds," yet in fact they had made $7,757,103 gross, paying a tax on *net* proceeds of $682.

The Anaconda Company, he pointed out, had paid no tax at all on net proceeds. He proposed a ten-cents-per-ton coal tax and then turned his attention to the Anaconda Company. He granted in fairness to the mining interests that they paid heavy taxes on surface value and on improvements, but what of the real wealth—the copper, gold, silver, lead, etc.? On this vast wealth *all the metaliferous mines in Montana* had paid an average of but $47,831 a year for the preceding five years. Certainly, said Dixon, ". . . no sane man would want to see [this industry] hampered in any way by unjust legislation or inequitable taxation . . . [but] I do not believe that under our present system of taxing the 'net proceeds' our metaliferous mining industry bears its rightful burden of government in Montana," and he recommended a license tax ". . . of the equivalent value of the present 'net proceeds' tax and also a change in the present law so as to equalize the 'net proceeds' tax over a five-year period." In fact, this left unaltered the unworkable net-proceeds basis for an equitable tax.

In dead silence, he went on to recommend a one-cent gasoline tax, an increased automobile license tax (there were 60,000 automobiles in Montana), the doubling of filing and recording fees in counties, the reorganization of "government bodies" to effect economies, the stringent consolidation of proliferating boards and bureaus, the commission form of

257

government for counties, and amendments to the Workman's Compensation Act, which would double the compensation (limited then to two weeks for medical and hospital services and to $50).

He wanted legislative reapportionment (which did not come until 1965), the redistricting of the Congressional districts (badly out of proportion *vis à vis* the population even in 1920), and he wanted the creation of a state purchasing agent, ". . . purchasing now being done by dozens of people, acting on their own . . . with no common purpose."

There were many other recommendations for reform and streamlining, some of which, very slowly over the succeeding years, have been accomplished. Many of Dixon's proposals of 1921 took years to adopt and implement—and others are still being studied.

Tucked into the middle of his report was the most volatile and fearsome of all his proposals. He wanted to establish a tax commission. "Neither you nor I," he said, "have the knowledge nor the technical information nor training to work out any coordinated system of taxation . . . equitable taxation is so important and far reaching, so vitally affecting every industry, community and person, that it should receive the earnest attention of this body." He wanted three members with six-year terms, appointed by the governor and removable by him. Such a body could be only advisory to the already existent State Board of Equalization, but what he wanted was trained and independent tax experts chosen not "by the haphazard selection of a primary election," and thus subject to political pressures, but men with expertise.

"Let all of us," he concluded, ". . . eliminate the petty things of politics and partisanship and work together in a sincere spirit of doing the bigger things for Montana."

At least it may be said that most of the newspapers recognized the significance of the message. Six dailies printed the text in full. The Billings *Gazette*, whose editor, John Edwards, was an old Dixon enemy, printed the message of Wyoming's governor instead.

Editorial comments were another matter. The Company press emphasized only that Dixon proposed drastically to increase taxes. A few papers expressed surprise at the lack of partisanship in the address. Will Campbell predictably warned against "radical remedies." The Anaconda *Standard* rallied against additional taxation of the state's "poor struggling industries."

Yet it is true that the Company press had obviously determined not to launch their campaign on the basis of the message itself. There was plenty of time to do so in the context of the bills which would give the message concrete form. In the meantime, the Company lobbyists set to work. They were, of course, often indistinguishable from the legislators themselves, since, indeed, many of them *were* legislators. The Silver Bow County contingent, for instance, could always be counted on to vote as a pro-Company bloc.

Lobbying in the Montana legislature was part art, part cold cash, part rubber-hose bludgeoning, and part cajolery, all of which was mixed with a perpetual stag drinking room, prohibition notwithstanding. The Company ran the only legislative information agency that existed, a service rendered gratis to all senators and representatives. The exact status of any bill at any moment could immediately be ascertained simply by asking the appropriate Company lobbyist. They also provided, gratis, a bill-writing service—and any legislator who wanted a bill drawn up had merely to outline his desires to the appropriate Company lobbyist and the finished product was delivered, often within a matter of hours.

Lobbyists (who were not themselves legislators) were Republicans, Democrats, or Independents—take your choice. They were ubiquitous but not egregious; they were informed, skilled, and their resources were unlimited—so was their resourcefulness. By far the best parliamentarians available were the Company lobbyists.

Not often, but occasionally, they were caught off guard and a bill would hit the floor and come to a vote without the house or senate having been briefed. It was then a source of great amusement to "legislature watchers" to observe the heads swing toward the gallery (where Company men were always posted) so that the signal could be given.[2]

Company lobbyists were of two kinds: "permanent" and "biennial." The "permanents" spent full time, twelve months a year, at the job. The tempo of their jobs picked up several months before every primary election, accelerated after the general election, and reached full scope at the session. The "permanents" all worked directly for the Company or a subsidiary, and most of them had official titles with A.C.M. They compiled the extensive dossiers which the Company kept on all legislators.

The "biennialists" were hired just for the session and for specific and more parochial roles. They were usually attorneys, and they were well paid with unlimited expense accounts.

Although the approaches and devices of lobbying were varied, imaginative, and myriad, one of the standard methods employed (which was rendered enormously effective be

[2] For a very amusing account of Company lobbying, see John M. Schiltz, "Montana's Captive Press," *Montana Opinion*, April, 1957, 195.

cause of the Company's almost total control of the press) was to introduce extraneous bills and then devise interminable debate and extensive press coverage of same. This served three purposes: it confused the inexperienced legislator as to the proper priority of things; it enabled the press to attack or laud specific legislators (or the governor) on matters unrelated to anything that really mattered; it hoodwinked the public and covered the legislative scene with a cloud of obfuscatory verbiage.[3]

Although the Company applied this form of lobbying with decreasing frequency after the mid-1930's, it was one of the truly effective devices used against Dixon. Its fulcrum was, of course, the press. Behind the scenes Company lobbyists were fighting Dixon's proposals with all the varied armaments in their arsenal. But the people who read the newspapers were hardly aware that the session was involved in fundamental economic matters at all.

Dixon's revenue measures were quickly buried in committees and there was thereafter an almost complete newspaper blackout concerning them. The exceptions were Campbell's Helena *Independent* and the Butte *Miner*, which attacked all of Dixon's tax proposals as unjust and unnecessary. The *Miner* said, "It is not more taxes the people want, but less . . . what the people have been expecting is the institution of drastic measures of economy and not the imposition of additional taxes."

3 Thus in the early 1950's, when fiscal matters were again critical, the legislation of the moment seemed to be: (1) the Bow and Arrow Bill, which sought to set a deer season for bow hunters, (2) the Peyote Bill, which sought to legalize the use of peyote (an extract of cactus) in Indian religious ceremonies, and (3) the Ham Bill, which sought to give amateur radio buffs the radio call number as it appeared on their license plates. The big issue in the 1968 session was the Bingo Bill, which sought to outlaw bingo at church socials and private clubs.

Dixon's Republican enemies, E. J. Donlan of Missoula (an old and trusted Company man), John Edwards of Rosebud, E. J. Booth of Fallon, and T. O. Larson of Teton were all experienced legislators of long tenure. They formed the hard core of those who held up the proposals in committee, arranged for crippling amendments, or engineered outright defeat. The income tax was simply defeated; the coal tax was lowered to five cents per ton; the oil tax was cut to one per cent, the net-proceeds tax was altered in form not at all, but was increased to a negligible extent. The critical Tax Commission Bill was decisively defeated. Dixon's suggestion for constitutional amendments as a method in lieu of statutory changes was completely snowed under. It was, said the *Miner*, "an unwarranted attack on the Ark of the Covenant."

In short, Dixon's legislative program might just as well never have been conceived. The press had given overwhelming coverage to a loyalty oath bill for teachers, a movie censorship bill (introduced by Missoula's anti-Dixon E. J. Donlan), and the so-called "snooping bill" creating special agents under the attorney general to aid in enforcing prohibition "and all other laws" (it created, in fact, a state police force). Many other foolish and irrelevant bills got widespread and detailed press coverage; Dixon's veto of such legislation got no coverage at all.

Dixon's very substantial proposals for economy in state, county, and municipal government received short shrift and were never mentioned in the press at all. His proposals for reapportionment and redistricting never got out of committee. Dixon's program was not only butchered, it was desiccated and buried.

Dixon's reaction to what must have been an enormously discouraging initial mauling was promptly to call a special session of the legislature. As was his right, he limited the considerations of that session to fiscal matters only.

One can only speculate as to his reasons for calling the special session. Such sessions were notoriously dangerous. Few governors had called them. The tenor of the regular session could hardly have changed. The probable reason is that he sought to build a case for 1922 and a more amenable group of legislators. He could hardly have been motivated by the prospects of a better press, since he knew full well that the special session would only feed the fires of a press clearly geared to an anti-Dixon campaign already virulent.

But Dixon was a man full of surprises. His friend, Rae Logan, on recalling that period, remarked, "Well, he did it because it was right and necessary. What other motivation did he need?"

His message to the special session was also surprising. He congratulated the members on their hard work on seven hundred bills in the regular session. He said he thought, however, "better work might be done and more intelligent conclusions arrived at . . . when our work is limited to the consideration of these [fiscal] matters only."

He pointed out that new revenue from all the sources could not exceed $580,000 for 1921, which was clearly insufficient. And he set before them his same fiscal program—which they had just emasculated. He finished by saying: "I have no mental reservations but that the Legislature wants to work out these questions in a spirit of fairness and looking only for the truth in the matters involved . . . this is a government 'of the people, by the people, and for the people.' . . . Whenever we shall have departed from that theory of public conduct this government will, surely, soon perish from the face of the earth."

263

The press went into a paroxysm of criticism over the special session and of Dixon. This time they zeroed in on the tax commission proposal (by far the most dangerous to the Company) and for the full term of the session (seventeen days) excoriated Dixon. The Billings *Gazette* said that he had "disgraced" the state, that his "effrontery" was appalling, that he was the "champion doublecrosser of the U.S." The daily *Missoulian* spoke of "criminal waste" and said that the calling of the session was "a disastrous and wasteful experience." The Butte *Miner* called Dixon's proposals the "most vicious laws ever introduced in a legislature of this commonwealth."

Miles Romney, still satirical and puckish, praised Dixon in Hamilton's *Western News* for "fighting every inch of the way" and exposing the "big tax dodgers and their interlocking lobby." Dixon had, said Romney, torn the mask from the "kept press" which "has blinded and fooled the people for so long." But the circulation of the *Western News* was less than one thousand.

Out of the session, Dixon got an oil tax, a shadow of an inheritance tax, and nothing else except a great tonnage of bad press publicity. He emerged in the "kept press," and those papers always affiliated with (and undoubtedly subsidized by) the Company press[4] as, to use their own words: "Spineless Joe," "vindictive," "opportunistic," "radical," "indiscreet," "a fool," "a sophist," "a liar," and similar sundry colorful characterizations.

It should be noted (nor did it surprise many Montanans)

---

[4] Small weeklies and county papers were almost wholly sustained by county and city legal notices and by job printing, the former put out on annual bids, the latter dependent upon rates. The Company handled recalcitrant county papers by moving in with absurdly low bids for legal printing and with job-printing rates which could put the small papers quickly out of business.

that immediately after the special session the Anaconda Company closed its mines and smelters. They did not bother to point out that their stocks of copper were huge and that the price of copper, in any event, was low. Without comment, they simply shut down—and they stayed shut down for nine months. It is probable that most Montanans got the message.

The press campaign against Dixon did not wane. It increased both in invective and intensity. The governor could make no move that was not construed as sinister and extravagant. One of the hot issues which kept him constantly embroiled with the press was his firing of Frank Conley, the warden of the state prison. Dixon believed that Conley had made off with nearly $200,000 of state funds. Since Conley was himself a power in Company politics, the result was an utterly infuriated attack on Dixon. The battle was protracted and extraordinarily bitter.

The *Western News* pointed out that on a salary of four thousand dollars a year Conley had amassed a fortune of nearly a half million dollars. And Romney, of the *News*, was one of the few editors who pointed out that the governor had a perfect right to remove a warden even without cause. For a year and a half the Conley case raged in the press. Will Campbell's Helena *Independent* went so far as to fabricate anti-Dixon, pro-Conley stories whose falsehood was so patent that even other Company papers had to deny their authenticity. It mattered not a whit to Campbell, who promptly invented others.

In the end, Conley was acquitted in district court in a juryless trial before Judge A. J. Horsky. The issue on which Horsky decided the case was apparently not whether Conley had, indeed, bilked the state of vast sums, but rather that none of Conley's activities in running the prison had, in fact, violated any statute, *per se*. It was later established that to run the prison under Conley's last year as warden had cost the state $324,428. Under Dixon's new appointee, the prison had operated for $177,478—a difference of $147,058 in one year. But, in fact, the guilt or innocence of Conley had never really been the issue. The object was to "get Dixon" and the Conley case helped. Economy of this sort troubled Campbell's Helena *Independent* not at all. What was really happening, according to the *Independent*, was simply that Dixon was turning prisoners loose—"slackers, seditionists, highwaymen, rapists, porch climbers, and jail-breakers."

Issue after issue was either invented or made to seem significant, to Dixon's detriment, as the months wore on. Ordinarily initiated by the Helena *Independent*, they were either run simultaneously by or reprinted later in the Butte *Miner*, the Anaconda *Standard*, the *Daily Missoulian*, and the Billings *Gazette*. Frequently they also ran in the independent but anti-Dixon *Great Falls Tribune* and *Bozeman Chronicle*. Only the Helena *Record-Herald,* Romney's little *Western News*, and the *Miles City Star* sought to refute the Company press. But the Company covered the state with a heavy and seamless blanket of anti-Dixon sentiment.

In 1922, Dixon thus sought to go directly to the people with his program. But no audience, however full the hall, could match the audience reached by the Company press. In 1922, anti-Dixon stories and editorials were not merely occasional—they were daily. Reading the Company papers for this period one is struck not only by the vast quantity of anti-Dixon material, but by the extraordinary vitriol and invective employed and by the almost complete disregard for even the most elementary facts. Much of what Dixon was accused of being and doing, he could neither have been nor done had he wanted to. Even the anti-Dixon *Great Falls Tribune* was driven to saying that "almost no heed is given to telling the truth. . . . This is not good newspaper work."

The legislative session which convened on January 1, 1923, was presented with essentially the same charge by Dixon as that of 1921. Again he reviewed the cold facts; again he was coolly nonpartisan; again he asked for tax reform and a tax commission. The complexion of that legislature was slightly different. There were fewer Republicans and more Democrats. Some of Dixon's old enemies were gone. But there were new ones to take their places. Dixon pointed out that while the production of the metal mines in 1922 had totaled more than twenty million dollars, all the mines together had paid, on the basis of the net-proceeds tax system, only $13,559. He advocated the enactment of a license tax of twelve cents a ton on gross tonnage. He did not get it. Like its counterpart in 1921, the legislature of 1923 was tightly controlled.

Dixon's term of office ran out, grimly and under the pressures of unrelieved and unremitting Company attack. But he girded himself nonetheless for the campaign of 1924. He prepared an initiative—Initiative Number 28, which, under the constitution, he had the undeniable right to do on the basis of that section which provided for the imposition of license taxes. Scheduled for presentation to the voters in the general election of 1924, Initiative 28 provided for a graduated levy upon the gross production of any mine, ranging from .25 of one per cent to one per cent. Mines producing less than $100,000 gross per year were exempted. Then he set about campaigning.

The campaign was hard, grim, and unrelenting. Dixon received no support from either Walsh or Wheeler—indeed, they supported his opponent, John E. "Honest John" Erickson. And there was the press.

Joseph M. Dixon was defeated by "Honest John" Erickson, 88,801 to 74,126. But, *mirabile dictu*, Initiative 28 passed. The Company had made a terrible tactical blunder. So preoccupied were they with Dixon, the man, the archfiend, the spendthrift, that they distracted the voters from Dixon's issue, the initiative, and in a record turnout of some 170,000 voters, it passed by 20,000 votes.

Dixon said, "In the years to come the people of Montana will gradually realize the great step forward which has been taken toward equalizing the tax burden." From 1924 through the next several years, the gross-proceeds license tax brought into the state's coffers from $300,000 to $400,000 annually. Dixon was dead politically, but he had wrought the only real reform in Montana's economic structure since 1889. He had *not* equalized the tax burden, he had failed in almost all his endeavors. He left office under so dark a cloud that the rest of his life (he died in 1934) was colored by the events of those four bitter years. The result was a kind of historical blackout of the man and his endeavors. Historical revisionists, with the benefit of perspective, have often, if not usually, resurrected the reputations of fine public men who tried but failed. This did not happen to Dixon.[5] The average Montanan, even those who are students of the state's history, know little of Dixon's travail, his remarkable insight, his steady courage and his refusal to knuckle under. His name is lost in the long list of mediocre (or worse) chief executives who preceded and

5 Hopefully it will when Karlin's full and detailed biography (see footnote 1) is published. He is praised briefly in Joseph Kinsey Howard's *Montana, High, Wide, and Handsome* and several fine articles by Karlin (unfortunately in obscure publications) intimate his greatness.

came after him. Montana is usually equated with Clark, Daly, Heinze, Walsh, and Wheeler. Dixon's name not only belongs among them, it properly belongs at the top of the list.

But what of Wheeler? After his resounding defeat for the governorship in 1920, Wheeler did some prolonged thinking. He was not unaware that all the Company guns were trained on Dixon. He knew that the Company would make stringent efforts in 1922 to unify the Democratic party as an antidote to Dixon's control of the Republicans. But he needed Walsh's support. He needed, at a minimum, Company neutrality, preferably their support.

Walsh was dubious about Wheeler's candidacy for the Senate. He felt that Wheeler was too ebullient, too prone to transforming "meaningless expressions of courtesy [on the Company's part] into promises of support." But, having kept close watch of Dixon's struggle with the Company, he also thought that their experiences with Dixon "may have made them wondrous kind toward him [Wheeler]."

Wheeler was sure of it. He had had a talk with Larry Dobell, editor of the Butte *Miner* and, as he reported to Walsh, "He was more interested in the legislature than he was in a candidate for the United States Senate."

To clear matters up, Wheeler told the Non-Partisan League, and reported to Walsh, that ". . . under no circumstances would I run in the event they endorsed me." Wheeler knew, in any event, that the league's power was fast diminishing. Walsh was convinced, and he threw his full support to his old friend.

The campaign was lackluster; the old Wheeler was gone. The Butte *Miner*, which had once reserved its shrillest invectives for "Bolshevik Burt," now described him "as between radicalism and conservatism . . . neutral." His position, said

269

editor Dobell, "could probably be described as progressive." Wheeler was even endorsed by his old enemies, J. Bruce Kremer and S. V. Stewart. The Democrats were united, and Wheeler won by a plurality of nearly 18,000 votes.

Wheeler's own analysis of his victory in his autobiography[6] partly explains his success: "The Company strategists realized they could not expect to openly attack me and at the same time hope to achieve the Company's goal of electing a Democratic legislature which would defeat Governor Dixon's tax program." True. But Walsh was instrumental in effecting peace with the Company; Wheeler disowned Non-Partisan League support and left the Company strictly alone during his campaign.

From 1922 to 1946, Wheeler had a distinguished career in the Senate. In the latter year, he was defeated in the primary, in spite of strong Company support, by a young unknown, Leif Erickson—probably because he had been a staunch isolationist before the war.

Like Walsh, Wheeler, after 1922, played his politics cautiously and conservatively in Montana. He was a good senator, maybe even a great one. But in furious contention with Franklin Roosevelt, which began in 1933, he slipped consistently from liberalism to conservatism.

What of the other "bright young lights" as of the teens and early twenties? Maybe what Joseph Kinsey Howard said of Sam C. Ford could, to some extent, be said of them all. Quoting unidentified "liberal critics," Howard wrote: "Ford . . . is like Wheeler, a tired radical . . . and he tired, they added bitterly, with phenomenal rapidity."[7] Ford was elected gov-

---

[6] *Yankee from the West*, with Paul Healy (Doubleday, 1962).

[7] "The Decline and Fall of Burton K. Wheeler," *Harper's Magazine*, March, 1947.

ernor for two terms in 1940; Wellington Rankin, after his defeat for attorney general in 1924, never regained public office in spite of repeated attempts. He soon became an avowed conservative. His sister, Jeannette, served in Congress from 1916 to 1918 and from 1941 to 1943. She voted against America's entry into both wars, but always seemed distracted by irrelevancies.

And so the challenge ended. Locked in, beset with depression, the gray thirties saw governors and legislators come and go—almost faceless, essentially voiceless.

The Progressives had come, they had fought, they had almost always lost—and then they went. Montana was in for a long sleep.

Someday someone will write a monograph on that long sleep: Montana in the 1930's and 1940's. But it is apt to be a dull monograph. The New Deal came, the New Deal went, the war came, the war went. What the nation did, Montana did. Perhaps a fillip here, a fillip there. Still, what it *really* was was twenty years of deep somnolence.

XI. THE GREAT GRAY BLANKET: THE CAPTIVE PRESS

> In my opinion, the Company has a perfect right to be as big as it wants to be; it has a right to lobby; it has a right to influence; it has a right to negotiate. It has the right to do everything legal of which I am aware, except that it has no right to own, edit and publish bad newspapers, and this it does.
>
> John M. Schiltz, "Montana's Captive Press," *Montana Opinion*, 1956.

EXACTLY when and why the Company press decided to withdraw from the "arena" will probably never be determined. By the mid-nineteen thirties, however, it was an accomplished fact. Gone were the blasting editorials, the diatribes, the big black alliterative headlines. Someone, somehow, even pulled the fangs of Will Campbell.

If the vituperation was gone, so was aggressive reporting and imaginative writing. So was the thorough coverage of local and state news which did not affect the Company. Talent departed along with invective. The Company simply dropped a great, gray blanket over Montana.

Maybe, indeed, the Company was only reacting to the times (which were also gray) and to the fact that no one and nothing appeared on the horizon to threaten them. The Dixons, Walshes, Wheelers, and Rankins were gone. The people were preoccupied with the Depression. And there was an undeniable and very widespread disenchantment with political remedies offered for economic ills. The Non-Partisan League was an anachronism. Labor in the thirties in Montana was often "radical," but it was increasingly transient. It was a buyer's market which, more than anything else, accounted for labor's impotence in the mines and woods camps.

Whether the press reflected the times or whether the Company simply spiked the guns because they were no longer needed is an imponderable. It does not really matter, because the effect was the same—an entire body politic, an entire community essentially without a press at all.

The fact is, no one knew at any given time how many newspapers the Company owned or controlled. Not until the year 1951 were any reliable figures available. And there is evidence that between 1900 and 1951 the Company dealt in newspapers as a trader might deal in commodities.

The "Company press" was criticized both inside and outside Montana from the turn of the century to the date of the sale of the papers in June, 1959. But no one was quite sure of what the "Company press" consisted.

Upton Sinclair guessed (in shocked amazement) in 1919 that the Company owned or controlled all but two of the newspapers in the state.[1] He was wrong, but he used the best figures he had for an educated guess.

Oswald Garrison Villard in *The Nation* in 1931 admitted that there was no way to "get at" the actual situation of Company ownership via accurate figures but he felt that the influence of the Company on the entire press of the state was pervasive and corrupting.

---

[1] See Upton Sinclair, *The Brass Check* (Pasadena, 1919), p. 242.

In 1946, John Gunther in *Inside U.S.A.* said of the press situation in Montana: "It is unique in America"; and he guessed that the Company owned or controlled "seven of the fourteen dailies in the state," and added: "Why the Company thinks that such an antediluvian tactic of ownership of its own newspapers is a good idea remains a mystery to most experts in public opinion. . . ."

In the early 1950's, *Time* magazine sent a reporter to Montana to do an "in-depth study" of this "unique captivity." The reporter nosed around Montana for several weeks and, in final frustration, wired his editors that he could not do the story. It was too much, as he put it, like trying to "get in a solid blow in a battle against feathers."

A reporter from *The Denver Post*, Thor Severson, was less easily discouraged when he undertook the same task in 1952. Severson's series in the *Post* unfolded in the general milieu of his own wonderment. Montana was, he said, "the last outpost in America of feudal journalism." After describing the deadness, the grayness, the almost complete lack of state and local news coverage, Severson asked, "A twentieth century fantasy? No, this is Montana in 1952."[2] The papers, he said, not only failed to report the news, ". . . the Company papers deal in a sort of editorial Afghanistanism." It is all right to editorialize about robins, the springtime, or the affairs of Afghanistan. Just don't mention Montana.

But in spite of the criticisms offered by "outsiders," by outraged journalists in *The Nation, The New Republic, The London Economist*, and many other magazines, the most penetrating criticisms of the "gray blanket" came from Montanans themselves in the years from 1930 to 1959. These

2 *The Denver Post*, April 22, 1952.

critics sometimes expressed a certain nostalgia for the days when the Company press admitted that it was a "company press" and fired broadsides of abuse at its enemies. Listen to Lee Metcalf, associate justice of Montana's Supreme Court in 1952.[3] Company reporting, said Metcalf, was "never the mirror of actuality . . . only those events are reported which occur in the kind of society the editors would like to have in existence." It was not so much a distortion of the news, Metcalf observed, "as the failure to print all the news. And such failure is selective. . . . The reader senses it. And the danger is, he almost comes to accept it. Whatever the issues, whatever the facts—it is the responsibility of a responsible press to report them. . . ." Editorial policy? "Deliberately dull. Dull with a purpose. The strokes of the editorial pen are reserved lest troubled waters be stirred. *It is a dedication to the status quo* [italics mine]."

Listen to John M. Schiltz, Billings attorney and former state legislator: "One must wonder about what Anaconda could do for itself and Montana if it opened up its presses and let in some air and light . . . if it took advantage of its talent and money to spur community and state reforms; and if its editors were allowed a free rein. . . . If Anaconda is unable to recognize this need of a free press, but insists that it has Montana's welfare at heart, it should sell its papers."[4]

Richard M. Ruetten, in commenting on the "gray blanket" wrote, "The (earlier) vulgar commentary of company editors was slowly replaced by innocuous platitudes from anonymous figureheads. . . . Anaconda's papers became monuments of indifference. . . ."[5]

---

3 *Ibid.*
4 In *Montana Opinion*, June, 1956.
5 *The Call Number*, Fall, 1959 (University of Oregon Library).

In 1951 the Fairmont Corporation, a wholly owned subsidiary of the Anaconda Company, made application to the Federal Communications Commission for permission to purchase control of a radio station in Great Falls. The law and the commission required that Anaconda answer certain questions regarding its subsidiary. The Company divulged that the subsidiary owned all the stock of the Post Publishing Company (Butte *Daily Post*, evening); Standard Publishing Company (*Montana Standard*, Butte, morning); 66⅔ per cent of the stock of the Gazette Printing Company (*Billings Gazette*, morning and evening); 94.6 per cent of the Livingston Publishing Company (Livingston *Enterprise*, evening); all of the Missoulian Publishing Company (*Missoulian*, morning and *Sentinel*, evening); 72.49 per cent of the Montana Record Publishing Company (Helena, *Independent Record*, evening); 33⅓ per cent of the Western Montana Publishing Company (*Western News*, weekly, Libby); and 90 per cent of the Mineral Publishing Company (weekly, Superior). So as of 1951, there it was: total circulation of Company papers, 89,934; total circulation of all independent papers in the state, 69,552.

But protest roared in to the commission from Montana concerning the Company's proposed purchase of a radio station and the commission ordered a public hearing to be held in Great Falls. Needless to say, the prospect of the hearing did not receive much press coverage in Montana. Fairmont Corporation then petitioned the FCC for reconsideration for the purchase without a public hearing! In a brief which accompanied the petition, the president of Fairmont, Roy H. Glover, discussed newspaper policy and denied that there was censorship or that "news slants" or "editorials" were "pipelined" from headquarters to the papers. There *was*,

277

he said, a general policy: to avoid "yellow journalism," to run newspapers "which do not emphasize public scandals, misfortunes of local residents tending to bring them into disgrace or embarrassment," to "avoid local, petty quarrels." Glover said the object "is to place in the homes and business places of the readers, news and editorials that are fit to print and be consumed by the adults and children having access to their pages."

This petition by Fairmont Corporation was denied by the FCC and no public hearing was ever held. Glover's statement of ownership and his general outline of press policy, did, however, throw a small beam into the darkness. John M. Schiltz, in an exquisitely written article in *Montana Opinion*[6] in 1956, was the first to point out that "the fact of the matter is that the hirelings either don't know the policy or they are cheating on him a little" and, in instance after instance, Schiltz pointed out events of very genuine significance to the state which received very wide coverage in the independent papers and none at all in the "captive press." Far too often for coincidence, the events were related either directly or indirectly to Company interests.

Not only in their petition to the FCC, but in invariable answer to the invariable question, why does a copper company own newspapers, the Company had responded, "as a good business investment, that and nothing more." Maybe, remarked Schiltz, but figures supplied the secretary of state (Montana) by Fairmont Corporation for 1955, showed that for an investment of $1,139,000 the papers had netted

---

6 *Montana Opinion* was a short-lived quarterly (only four issues came out) which, like other publications of its kind, grew from the fact that ". . . we (the editorial board) are convinced that the perceptive Montanan is sick and tired of living without a candid and intelligent press." See Vol. I, No. I, "Statement of Intentions."

$16,700—or a return of .014 per cent on its investment. Not a very good return. And figures supplied the FCC showed that Fairmont had actually lost money in 1950. Schiltz concluded: "Bad journalism is almost incapable of documentation for yardsticks are arbitrary, if they exist at all; it's either good or it's bad and the Anaconda brand is bad. One never knows how bad until he sees other papers and survives the first shock of seeing controversy and news in print."

So, until 1959 when the Company at long last did sell the papers, the average Montanan saw his state only partially. It was fragmented—as the press saw it. He could not, indeed, even see his own town or valley in the actual terms of what was happening or what was needed or what was wrong. If he discovered these things at all, he did so on his own, in spite of, and not because of, the press. Unless, again, he served as his own reporter or investigator, he never knew what real issues faced the legislature or why—or even, indeed, how the legislature disposed of them—if it did.

Always there were small, independent papers, some "radical," some merely enraged. They came and went with regularity. None of them spoke to a significantly large constituency, except for the *Great Falls Tribune*, whose circulation in the 1950's was some 16,000. It was the one bright journalistic light in Montana—but it cast its beam into a very deep and palpable journalistic gloom.

Then on June 1, 1959, the Company announced the sale of all its papers in Montana. The purchaser was Leo P. Loomis, home base, Mason City, Iowa, and head of the Lee Newspapers, an independent, successful, Midwest chain. The Lee chain provided an early editorial guarantee: "We serve only one interest—the public. There were no strings attached to the sale of these newspapers. Our only obligations are to

279

our subscribers and our communities." But Montanans were wary. The Lee chain also announced that they were going to retain "the men and women who have worked conscientiously to develop your newspapers. . . . We have met many of them, and we plan to build on with this team." One professor of journalism at the University remarked, "With *this* team! Well, then, there goes the ball game!"

But, oddly, that was not the case. True, change in the newspapers came slowly and varied widely from paper to paper. But it came. For older Montanans, those who "grew up" in the 1930's and 1940's with the Company press, it is still amazing to pick up the daily *Missoulian*, for instance, and find it vehemently attacking the Anaconda Company for air and water pollution—or to find it investigating in detail why the lumber industry (vital to Missoula's economy) is doing so little to fight environmental degradation.

All of the Lee papers give comprehensive coverage to legislative matters, to local government, to school problems, in short, to the real problems which confront their communities.

The *Missoulian*, in particular, has come more and more to engage in "in-depth" investigations of Montana's racial problems (Indians), its lagging economy, and above all, environmental matters. Often, its editorial policy is openly opposed to the "interests"; the Company, the saw mills, pulp plants, and a timid U.S. Forest Service.

We will doubtless never know what precise considerations led the Company to sell its papers. But certainly somewhere behind the sale lay the factor of profound change in Montana and in the Company in the years subsequent to World War II.

XII. IT IS A LONG HAUL

> It would be pleasant to report that we expect Montana, at long last, to share fully in this national economy. But our guess is that it will not.
>
> *Montana Economic Study*, Bureau of Business Research, University of Montana

I

AS the population of America has become more homogeneous, as the ubiquitous TV antenna has spread American culture and "non-culture" into every corner of the land, one might expect old patterns, old curses, and old blessings to alter drastically. And, indeed, they have—so much so that some observers of the American scene believe that we are, in fact, undergoing a kind of social, political, and economic revolution.

Yet there is a fierce tenacity to old problems and old patterns. They are ingrained—and they are (or at least seem to be) utterly basic.

Since its inception, Montana has paid dearly for the high cost of space. It has paid for its distance from markets. It is a "raw materials" area, not a fabricating area. Its wealth in terms of minerals, timber, grass, and abundant water is enormous. But by the very nature of things the largest percentage of this wealth is not kept at home.

One would think that with the "shrinking" of the world and the country, Montana's position *vis à vis* the nation would change—a mile no longer being a mile but an inch. After all, it once took a month of the hardest kind of travel to reach Pittsburgh. Now it takes a day.

But an old economic pattern in Montana remains. It remains because we are dealing with relative matters. And we are, in many ways, still what we were—far from the axis of trade, huge, remote, and "exploited"—not by the evil designs of men, but because we grow what we grow and mine what we mine—and are what we are.

Economists, admittedly, do not measure everything nor do they presume to. But they can and do measure some very important things. And these measurable things often reflect on matters otherwise imponderable.

In the fall of 1970, the Bureau of Business Research at the University of Montana delivered to the state (the governor, the Department of Planning and Economic Development, and others) the *Montana Economic Study*. No such study of root economic facts had ever been made before and the year's effort, presided over by competent and experienced economists, produced some shocks.

The state is economically stagnant not merely in comparison to national norms and averages, but even in comparison to its neighbors, the northern Rocky Mountain states (Idaho, Wyoming, Utah, and Colorado).

One vital index of economic health is per capita personal income (i.e., total personal income divided by population). As of 1950, Montana stood a full 8 per cent above the national average. By 1968 it was 14 per cent *below* the national average. Moreover, projections to the year 1980 indicate a further decline to 21 per cent below the national average.

In the eighteen years between 1950 and 1968, Montana's population increased only 17 per cent—less than half as fast as its sister states; only slightly faster than half of the national rate. Employment increased only 14 per cent in Montana, while the nation's increased more than 33 per cent and the northern Rocky Mountain states more than 41 per cent.

These statistics constitute a grim enough picture as it is, but corollary calculations make it worse: the state's slow growth is essentially due to an out-migration of people, especially the young. Over the past decade net out-migration has averaged slightly more than 3,000 persons yearly. Why? Essentially because there is (and has been) a "job gap" in the state—a failure of jobs to increase commensurate with the "natural" growth of the state. Moreover, this out-migration has been heavily laden with young people. The consequence is that Montana is not only losing "the cream of the crop," but it is losing precisely those whom it has paid to educate in its institutions of higher learning.

Lest such a catalog of sorrows make economic doom seem imminent, let it be noted that for most of its history (since the mining rushes drew young men almost exclusively to the territory) this tendency toward the loss of the young has been periodically prevalent. Joseph Kinsey Howard spoke of the period subsequent to World War I and the loss of young men as having "changed the whole structure of the population." "The census chart," he wrote, "took on the appearance of a bull fiddle or an hour glass—wasp-waisted where it should have shown the 'earning group.' Within a few years Montana was transformed from a young people's state to a state of young children and old men and women."

Indeed, thoughtful Montanans (at least those over fifty) will probably not be shocked by the *Montana Economic Study* because many of them can remember when it was worse. When the whole nation was joyously upward bound in the 1920's, Montana was at rock bottom. The great Depression of the 1930's came as no shock to Montanans—we had

283

already had a decade's experience with bank failures, staggeringly low prices for cattle and wheat, an erratic and often depressed lumber industry, and sky-high unemployment rates.

But the *Economic Study* pricks many a balloon of bright, naïve hopes and dispels many loose-jointed arguments that Montana is on the hither edge of great economic prosperity. It brings one face to face with certain facts as hard as steel and as cold as ice.

Montana's decline in the vital areas of meaningful indicators (such as per capita income) is rooted in the nature of the state's industries, as well as in the factors of distance and the high cost of space. The state specializes (perforce) in only a few major export industries—all of which depend for stability on national or international markets: forest products, agriculture, mining, and railroading.

But, says the boom-dreamer, are we not rapidly diversifying? Are we not less dependent than we once were on these industries? Of course, but we are not "diversifying" at a rate sufficiently fast to overcome our slide downward, and while these big, primary industries today provide less than half the total jobs in the state, as *they* go, so goes the state. As the *Economic Study* put it, "they are the driving force behind economic growth (or decline)."

Behind that fact lies another: While America's economy has (with a few setbacks) boomed lustily since the end of World War II, *these* industries, agriculture, mining, forest products, and railroads have not. In every one of them employment has declined sharply since World War II. Or, to put it another way, the vast bulk of the increase in national primary employment in the United States came in manufacturing industries which are simply not important in Montana.

This root fact was somewhat offset by what the *Economic Study* terms "derivative" employment—jobs in industries catering to local markets and the "service industries": restaurants, barbershops, service stations, etc.

The *Economic Study*'s projections were based on studies by the National Planning Association, a private organization in Washington, D.C. The NPA predicts a very prosperous decade for the country as a whole. It sees nothing of the kind for Montana. It predicts a very slow absolute population growth—only 725,000 persons by 1980. While there is a chance that opportunities in mining may increase somewhat, agriculture and railroading will continue to slide. Balancing all factors, the projection for Montana is that total primary jobs will increase very little if at all and that per capita income (perhaps the most accurate measurement of over-all economic health) will have slipped from its present 14 per cent below the national average to 21 per cent below that average.

What to do? Can the economic trend be reduced or reversed? Is it inexorable and should Montanans, therefore, who *are* employed and *can* keep body and soul satisfactorily together simply relax and enjoy the extraordinary beauty of their land and the peculiar independence in their lives—and forget the whole business?

While the *Economic Study* presents possible and variable programs as palliative measures and while it contains a discussion of the pros and cons of faster growth, it says, "Economic growth or decline can change the character of an area drastically. Opinions differ widely as to whether the effects are good or bad, and we cannot settle that question." Indeed they cannot. Nor can anyone else. The matter is invincibly subjective.

285

But does the study hold out much hope that the trend can be reversed by action on the state level, that is by setting up a "climate" of taxation, advertising, promotion, and other enticements which will be effective? It does not. It states: ". . . the power of the state to influence the rate at which it grows without resorting to actions deleterious to the general welfare [such as abolishing all air and water pollution controls] are severely limited." The study does not assert that all state effort to influence economic development should be abandoned. It merely says that Montanans should recognize that state development policies have very limited effectiveness, primarily because the root of the problem lies too deeply buried in myriad interlocking factors of cost, distance, labor force, and national and international market conditions. States can do little to alter these root factors. But are there approaches which might be conceived for the alleviation of our economic stagnation or as palliatives? Let the report speak for itself:

> We think it would be a mistake for the state to set a single target for economic development policy in the coming decade, and that it would be particularly unrealistic to set a target such as the elimination of the job gap. Most goals are not exclusive and cannot be pursued single-mindedly. Given the uncertainties that must surround any projections, the limitations on the state's powers to promote growth, and the inability to assess fully and resolve in advance the potential conflicts between any particular kind of growth and other policy goals, setting a concrete goal in terms of, say employment in 1980, would probably result in undue pressures to accomplish what might well turn out to be the wrong task.

The *Montana Economic Study* will doubtless not please the director of the State Planning and Development Commission, unless, of course, he leans toward *ad hoc* approaches in any event. The study is apt to displease many politicians because in Montana as elsewhere, governors in particular, are apt to campaign on the promise of swift action aimed at improving economic conditions. The study will dismay booster groups everywhere. But there it is, and they will have to refute it or ignore it—which, in either case, will be difficult to do.

II

What then are we? We have reviewed seventy years in the history of a state during the course of which this "entity," this "thing," this "place" called Montana has been cyclically beaten, battered, and bruised. It has often been misgoverned, exploited, lied to, and lied about. It has suffered as "an outpost of feudal journalism"—the only state in the nation without an essentially free press. It has been visited by awesome drought, withering poverty, and genuine suppression of civil rights, riots, and lynchings. (It has been notable for legislative incompetence of lowest order, corporate arrogance of the highest order, corruption, and cynicism.) Now, in the midst of the most affluent period in the history of America, we have shared in that affluence only marginally, and there is abundant evidence that even that share will diminish.

This place is called "The Land of the Big Sky," and whatever else it had, it had elbow room, clean air, pristine rivers, and crystal lakes. But have we? Ask the resident of Missoula, that lush, green valley town, now often hidden entirely from view by the stinking, yellowish-gray smog of a pulp plant. Ask the resident of Columbia Falls where the effluent from an aluminum plant has yellowed every pine tree for miles around. Ask the resident of Billings where the stink of oil refineries stretches all the way to Laurel. Ask those dozens of groups of conservationists now locked in combat with the giant polluters if we really have a big sky—or if, indeed, in spite of the intensity of the fight of the environmentalists, we are *really* going to win *this* one. We have lost so many battles in the twentieth century. On what can they base their optimism concerning this one?

In so far as this study is a "portrait," looked at one way, it is like the portrait of Dorian Gray. Montana has rugged topographical features. One might be tempted to say that this shows that long ago it took a geological beating—and in many ways has been taking a beating ever since. But there are myriad angles from which to view a portrait. Lights and shadows change a visage. And it matters, too, if the viewer knows the subject intimately or not at all.

Consider then, *one* view of what Montana is and why. And consider it by standing back from the portrait and looking at it from a distance. Montana is a state with a rugged heritage which has also often been violent. It was a tough place to live for the Indians, the mountain men, the miners, the loggers, and the honyockers. But they lived in it—and most of them loved it. They did not have to live here. They chose to—or they left. And that is the way it is, in a way, today. What pulls people to this remote place when they could do better elsewhere? What keeps Montanans here who could better themselves economically by moving? What creates that strangely intense, often defensive, loyalty to a place? The answer is as varied as Montanans are varied. But somehow, mixed up in it all, are some common ingredients.

Maybe the only way really to see how meager a mark mankind has made on this land (in spite of smelters, pulp plants, and refineries) is to fly in a small plane, very slowly and at low altitude, over its length and breadth. Its wilderness areas are as large as some European countries—and wilderness areas aside, one can fly for mile after mile after mile, and see no road, no automobile, no town, no railroad track. East of the Continental Divide it is like the sea with the wind moving tawny grass like waves from horizon to horizon—and not a single mark of man. In the West the little geometric patterns of towns vanish if you look away for just a moment and they are swallowed up in the vast tumult of the mountains—those gigantic folds, layers, and gorges changing in the light, constantly shifting their enormity, organic, restless, and infinitely lonely. That is one way to look at the portrait of Montana. And that is one reason Montanans feel so strongly about their land.

Now, on an October day walk up a canyon in the Bitterroots—walk just a single mile and sit down. There will be a soft rustling of aspen, there will be a soft hushing in the tops of the tall pines—and no other sound—and no man has ever sat there before.

East or west there is that profound quietness lying just beneath the surface of the small sounds the land makes. And within twenty minutes of slow driving from any city in Montana, you are suddenly in it—and alone. It has always been there—and you feel it, that old, that primitive affinity for where you came from some limitless time ago.

The fact is that that is why the environmentalists in Montana will win. The battle is not really being fought in the laboratory or in the legislature or the courts—as other losing battles have been. This one is utterly visceral. If the fight against environmental degradation can be won anywhere, it will be won here—precisely because nowhere in America is that visceral relationship with the land more powerfully felt by those who live there. The projections of the *Montana Economic Study* extend to 1980. But there is something that needs consideration beyond that and behind that. Only in the last twenty years—or even less—have Americans challenged the automatic belief that symbiotically growth is good and good is growth. And so America grew by eating upon itself—by devouring space, by devouring land. But there is no more land; there is no more space to devour. So, what we have left of what we once had has suddenly become precious —just as any scarce commodity becomes precious. And it will become more and more so until it becomes infinitely precious because we cannot live without it.

Montana is graced with an abundance of that vanishing commodity. It cannot yet (if ever) be translated into dollars. It cannot be measured because it is a thing of the spirit. It cannot really be quantified because it is a quality.

If then, peering closely at the portrait, you see a face (as you will) which is battered and pitted, and twisted and worn —move back, stand back—and look again. You will see an important face—and the longer you look, the more beautiful it will become.

ADDITIONAL READING

This is not a bibliography. It is intended merely to guide readers who may wish to probe into matters more deeply to the best of the material which bears on the general subject. In the works cited by chapter here they will find further citations and, in many instances, such as in the case of master's theses, they will find exhaustive bibliographies. The works cited here are merely places to begin.

I have listed no newspapers here. I have mentioned a good many in the text. I have, nevertheless, made extensive use throughout this work of newspaper material. While good collections exist at the University of Montana, Missoula, and at Montana State University, Bozeman, the collection of the Montana Historical Society at Helena is one of the most complete in the West.

Background Reading

Several excellent works cover Montana's history up to the period of statehood (1889). See Merrill G. Burlingame, *The Montana Frontier*, Helena, State Publishing Company, 1942, and also J. M. Hamilton's, *From Wilderness to Statehood*, Portland, Binfords and Mort, 1957.

In the line of anthologies (which extend beyond 1889) there are also two excellent works: Joseph Kinsey Howard's *Montana Margins: A State Anthology*, New Haven, Yale University Press,

1946, and *The Montana Past: An Anthology*, edited by Michael P. Malone and Richard B. Roeder, Missoula, University of Montana Press, 1969.

Two interpretive histories should also be consulted, Joseph Kinsey Howard's *Montana: High, Wide, and Handsome*, New Haven, Yale University Press, 1943, and K. Ross Toole's *Montana: An Uncommon Land*, Norman, University of Oklahoma Press, 1957. Both are critically interpretive. One can also find a wealth of information, though somewhat unevenly organized, in Merrill G. Burlingame's and K. Ross Toole's *History of Montana*, 3 vols., New York, The Lewis Publishing Company, 1957.

Perhaps the most penetrating study of the Great Plains area, next to Walter Prescott Webb's classic, *The Great Plains*, is Carl F. Kraenzel's *The Great Plains In Transition*, Norman, University of Oklahoma Press, 1955. Kraenzel was for many years a rural sociologist at Montana State University so that eastern Montana (for once) gets full treatment in the general context of the Great Plains.

Chapter Readings

Chapter I, *The Setting*. The figures and statistics are drawn from the census of 1900 or from the various Polk city directories of that year. The material was organized from these and other sources into a 122-page compendium of statistical information entitled "Montana: 1900–1910," by Robert Horn, as a work-study project under my guidance in the summer of 1968. This very useful document is in the Archives, University of Montana, Missoula.

Chapters II and III, *It is Still Not Too Late: Go West* and *The Boom and the Bust*. The honyocker period in the state's history has still not been as thoroughly done as the subject warrants. One must, I think, begin with a kind of classic, Mary Wilma Hargreaves, *Dry Farming in the Northern Great Plains, 1900–1925*

292

(Cambridge, Harvard University Press, 1957). This massive study is indispensable to an understanding of the national significance of the period. It is vastly detailed—so much so that one can readily get lost in hundreds of graphs, charts, and tables. Indeed, it is more a reference work than a book. It is difficult to use, too, because Mrs. Hargreaves draws almost no conclusions and makes no judgments. She simply presents pounds of raw materials, facts, and figures. It is, in any event, by far the most thorough study of the subject.

Charles Dalich's "Dry Farming Promotion in Eastern Montana (1907–1916)," master's thesis, University of Montana, 1968, is a good study of the period of promotion. It is particularly useful because of his widespread use of the newspapers of the area and time.

Also useful are the papers of Governor S. V. Stewart, in the Archives of the University of Montana. He was governor during this critical period and his papers are revealing, particularly as illustrative of just how impotent state government was in the face of this crisis.

On reclamation and irrigation prior to the dry-land phenomenon, see Stanley Davison, "Hopes and Fancies of the Early Reclamationists" in *Historical Essays on Montana and the Northwest*, edited by John Welling Smurr and K. Ross Toole (Helena, Western Press, 1957), pp. 204–23.

For the best picture of the honyocker himself see Joseph Kinsey Howard, *Montana: High, Wide, and Handsome* (New Haven, Yale University Press, 1943), Chapters XVII and XVIII.

Almost nothing has been done on county-splitting except for a short section in Howard's *Montana*. The subject needs and deserves intensive study. Hassing, Joanne Marie (Griffin), "The Creation of Petroleum County: A Case Study in 'County Busting,' " master's thesis, University of Montana Political Science Department, 1966, is good.

The banking catastrophe has been treated in some detail by

Howard (Chapter XX) but he did not have access to crucial facts and makes some critical errors both of fact and interpretation. One should balance Howard's contentions with Don Elliot's "Commercial Bank Failures in Montana, 1920–1926," master's thesis, University of Montana, 1967. Elliot had abundant material from the Archives of the Federal Reserve Bank of Minneapolis itself—as well as access to banking research in Montana which Howard did not use.

One should also read with care Clarence W. Groth's "Sowing and Reaping: Montana Banking 1910–1925" in *Montana the Magazine of Western History*, Autumn, 1970. Also of significance is correspondence between myself and sundry bankers at the Federal Reserve Bank, Minneapolis, now in the University Archives, Missoula.

Chapter IV. *The Great Shutdown*. There is abundant material on the Great Shutdown and the War of the Copper Kings. Among the best are Carl Burgess Glasscock, *The War of the Copper Kings: Builders of Butte and Wolves of Wall Street,* (Indianapolis, N.Y., The Bobbs-Merrill Co., 1935); Christopher Powell Connolly, *The Devil Learns to Vote, The Story of Montana*, (New York, Covici, Friede, 1938); Sarah McNelis, *Copper King at War; the Biography of F. Augustus Heinze* (Missoula, University of Montana Press, 1968); Thomas W. Lawson, *Frenzied Finance: Vol. I, The Crime of Amalgamated*, (New York, The Ridgway-Thayer Co., 1905); K. Ross Toole, "The Genesis of the Clark-Daly Feud," *The Montana Magazine of History*, I (April, 1951), 21–33; K. Ross Toole, "When Big Money Came to Butte; The Migration of Eastern Capital to Montana," *Pacific Northwest Quarterly*, 44 (January, 1953), 23–29; K. Ross Toole, "Marcus Daly: A Study of Business in Politics," master's thesis, University of Montana, 1948.

Chapter V, *Gibraltar Laid Low*. Fundamental to an understanding of Butte's chaotic labor history is Vernon Jensen's

Heritage of Conflict: Labor Relations in the Nonferrous Metals Industry up to 1930, (Ithaca, Cornell University Press, 1950); Robert Emylyn Evans, "Montana's Role in the Enactment of Legislation Designed to Suppress the Industrial Workers of the World," master's thesis, University of Montana, 1964, is succinct and excellent.

The best and by far the most thorough work in this area, however, has been done by Arnon Gutfeld in several works. First, "The Butte Labor Strikes and Company Retaliation During World War I," master's thesis, University of Montana, 1967; Arnon Gutfeld, "The Ves Hall Case, Judge Bourquin, and the Sedition Act of 1918," *Pacific Historical Review*, XXXVII (May, 1968), 163–78; Arnon Gutfeld, "The Speculator Disaster in 1917; Labor Resurgence of Butte, Montana," *Arizona and the West*, II (Spring, 1969), 27–38; Arnon Gutfeld, "The Levine Affair: A Case Study in Academic Freedom," *Pacific Historical Review*, XXXIX (February, 1970), 19–37. Mr. Gutfeld's forthcoming book-length study of Montana during World War I should fill in what few blank places remain. Mr. Gutfeld's scholarship is impeccable and he writes concisely and well.

For an excellent study of the Great Lumber Strike of 1917, see Benjamin G. Rader, "The Montana Lumber Strike of 1917," *Pacific Historical Review*, XXXVI (May, 1967), 189–207.

Chapter VI, *Panic: The Early War Years*. Much information on this subject is available in Gutfeld's work as well as in the work of Evans cited above. Gutfeld's is the more sophisticated. One should by all means read Burton K. Wheeler (with Paul Healy), *Yankee From the West: the Candid Turbulent Life Story of the Yankee-born U.S. Senator From Montana* (Garden City, N.Y., Doubleday, 1962), which is delightful reading as well as informative. Indispensable is Kurt Wetzel, "The Making of an American Radical: Bill Dunne in Butte," master's thesis, University of Montana, 1970, which is a fine study of Dunne and the Butte *Bulletin*. Again see Rader's work on the lumber strike.

295

Chapter VII, *The Inquisition*. For this period there is no substitute for the records themselves. Those records and verbatim testimony before the State Council as well as correspondence from and to the County Councils are in the Archives of the State Historical Society, Helena. A good, solid survey of the subject can be found in Nancy Fritz, "The Montana Council of Defense," master's thesis, University of Montana, 1966. See also Wheeler's *Yankee From the West* and Gutfeld on Bourquin. One should also see those portions of the S. V. Stewart Papers (Archives, University of Montana) which apply to the Council. Further, one should read the *Bulletin* of W. F. Dunne, for there is no substitute for Dunne's own style.

Chapter VIII, *The University and the Company*. On Levine, see Gutfeld, cited above, which is by far the most complete study of the Levine case. Levine, who died in 1970, kept up a voluminous correspondence with Gutfeld. See also K. Ross Toole, "The Anaconda Copper Mining Company," doctoral dissertation, University of California at Los Angeles, 1954; Joseph Kinsey Howard in *Montana: High, Wide, and Handsome* has a brief sketch of the subject. As for the Fisher case, the only reliable account—and it is excellent and thorough—is Sheila Stearns, "The Arthur Fisher Case," master's thesis, University of Montana, 1969. See also, particularly concerning Chancellor Elliott's role, Frank K. Burrin, "Edward Charles Elliott, Educator," doctoral dissertation, Purdue University, 1956. Vignettes of Levine and Fisher appear in H. G. Merriam's *History of the University of Montana* (Missoula, University of Montana Press, 1970). No study of the Levine case could be complete without a reading of Levine's own book, *The Taxation of Mines in Montana* (New York, B. W. Huebsch, 1919).

Chapter IX, *The Progressives Make Their Move*. A two-volume history of Joseph M. Dixon by Jules Karlin, University of Montana, is nearing completion. Until these volumes, based on

Dixon's papers in the University Archives, are published, nothing really definitive can be said about Dixon.

One should begin with Dixon's own two State of the State messages: Montana: Messages of the Governors, 1921–1923. Proceed to Jules Alexander Karlin, "Progressive Politics in Montana" in a *History of Montana* (2 vols.) by Merrill Burlingame and K. Ross Toole (New York, Lewis Publishing Company, 1956). See also Joseph Kinsey Howard, *Montana: High, Wide, and Handsome*; also Shirley DeForth "The Montana Press and Governor Joseph M. Dixon, 1920–1922," master's thesis, University of Montana, 1959. From there on it is a question of piecing a picture of Dixon together from the several works on T. J. Walsh by J. Leonard Bates, *The Origins of the Teapot Dome; Progressives, Parties and Petroleum, 1909–1921* (Urbana, University of Illinois Press, 1963); "Senator Walsh of Montana, 1918–1924, A Liberal Under Pressure," doctoral dissertation, University of North Carolina, 1952; *Tom Walsh in Dakota Territory: Personal Correspondence of Senator Thomas J. Walsh and Elinor C. McClements* (Urbana, University of Illinois Press, 1966), and from Wheeler's work. My own picture of Dixon was greatly enriched by personal interviews with his close friend and counselor, Rae Logan of Charlo, Montana.

As for Wheeler, in addition to *Yankee from the West*, see Richard T. Ruetten, "Burton K. Wheeler, 1905–1925: An Independent Liberal Under Fire," master's thesis, University of Oregon, 1957; Richard T. Ruetten, "Burton K. Wheeler: A Progressive Between Wars," doctoral dissertation, University of Oregon, 1961; Richard T. Ruetten, "Senator Burton K. Wheeler and Insurgency in the 1920's," in *The American West, A Reorientation*, Gene Gressley, ed. (Laramie, University of Wyoming Publications, Vol. XXXII, 1966); Joseph Kinsey Howard, "The Decline and Fall of Burton K. Wheeler," *Harper's Magazine*, 195 (March, 1947), 226–36; Richard L. Neuberger, "Wheeler of Montana," *Harper's Magazine,* (May, 1940), 609–18; Catherine

Doherty, "The Court Plan, B. K. Wheeler, and the Montana Press," master's thesis, University of Montana, 1954; Joseph P. Kelly, "A Study of the Defeat of Senator Burton K. Wheeler in the 1946 Democratic Primary Election," master's thesis, University of Montana, 1959; Richard A. Haste, "What is Wheeler?," *American Review of Reviews*, October, 1924, 406–409; G. W. Johnson, "Wheeler Rides the Storm," *Colliers*, CXIV (July 8, 1944), 11ff; Richard L. Neuberger, "Wheeler Faces the Music," *Nation*, August 28, 1937, 216–20; Gordon Reid, "How They Beat Wheeler," *New Republic*, CXV (July 29, 1946), 99–101; Arnon Gutfeld, "The Speculator Disaster in 1917; Labor Resurgence at Butte, Montana," *Arizona and the West*, Vol. 11, No. 1 (Spring, 1969) 27–38.

Chapter XI, *The Great Gray Blanket: The Captive Press*. See Richard Reutten, "Anaconda Journalism: The End of an Era," *Journalism Quarterly*, XXXVII (Winter, 1960), 3–12; John M. Schiltz, "Montana's Captive Press," *Montana Opinion*, I (June, 1956), 1–11; Richard T. Ruetten, "Togetherness: A Look into Montana Journalism," *The Call Number*, XXI (Fall, 1959). One should also consult "The Captive Press," in K. Ross Toole's work "The Anaconda Copper Mining Company," doctoral dissertation, University of California, 1954. Other references are contained in the chapter itself.

Chapter XII, *It Is A Long Haul*. The figures and projections in this chapter are taken entirely from the summary of the *Montana Economic Study*. This research report, the first of its kind, was prepared by the School of Business Administration, Bureau of Business and Economic Research. The director of the study was Samuel B. Chase, Jr. Professor Chase had the help of four research associates, four research assistants, and one student.

INDEX

299